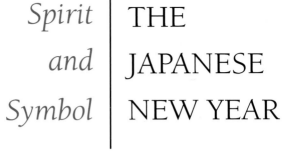

Spirit and Symbol

THE JAPANESE NEW YEAR

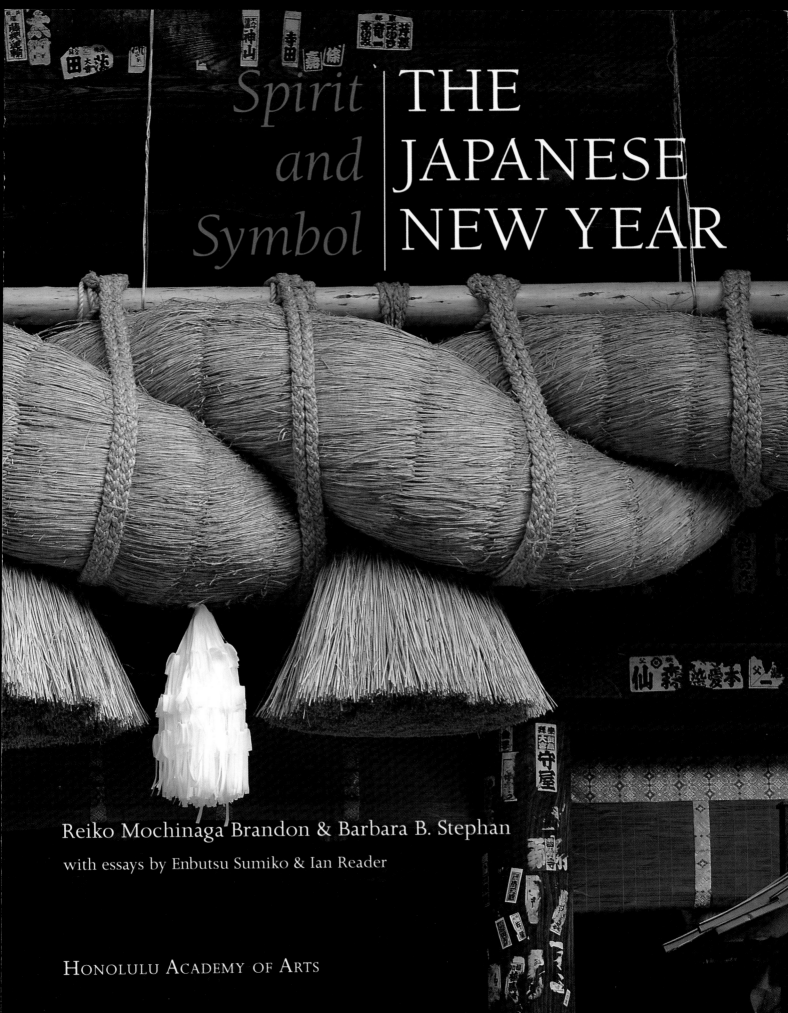

Spirit and Symbol

THE JAPANESE NEW YEAR

Reiko Mochinaga Brandon & Barbara B. Stephan

with essays by Enbutsu Sumiko & Ian Reader

HONOLULU ACADEMY OF ARTS

THIS PROJECT WAS MADE POSSIBLE WITH GENEROUS GRANTS FROM

The Japan Foundation Center for Global Partnership
 and
The Japan World Exposition Commemorative Fund

OTHER MAJOR SPONSORS

First Hawaiian Bank
Hawaii State Foundation on Culture and the Arts
Oceanic Cablevision & Nippon Golden Network

ADDITIONAL CORPORATE SPONSORS

Central Pacific Bank
City Bank
D/E Hawaii Joint Venture
The Dai'ei (USA), Inc.
Dennis Chevron Service
GTE Hawaiian Tel
Hazama Corporation
Ito-En (USA) Inc.
JTB Hawaii, Inc.
Mitsukoshi (USA), Inc.
Nippon Express Hawaii, Inc.
Nissan Motor Corporation in Hawaii, Inc.
Servco Foundation
Shimaya Shoten, Ltd.

ADDITIONAL GOVERNMENT SPONSOR

The National Endowment for the Arts

In-kind support was provided by Japan Airlines, All Nippon Airways, Outrigger Hotels Hawaii, and Hawaii Prince Hotel Waikiki

Published on the occasion of the exhibition
Spirit and Symbol: The Japanese New Year
organized by the Honolulu Academy of Arts
January 13 – February 27, 1994

Copyright © 1994 Honolulu Academy of Arts

LIBRARY OF CONGRESS CATALOGING-IN-PUBLICATION DATA

Spirit and symbol: the Japanese New Year / [by Reiko Mochinaga
    Brandon & Barbara B. Stephan; essays by Reiko Mochinaga
    Brandon...[et al.]]
        p.   cm.
        Includes bibliographical references and index.
    ISBN: 0-937426-24-5 (Honolulu Academy of Arts: hard)—
ISBN: 0-937426-25-3 (Honolulu Academy of Arts: pbk.)—
ISBN: 0-8248-1626-9 (University of Hawaii Press: hard)—
ISBN: 0-8248-1627-7 (University of Hawaii Press: pbk.)
        1. New Year—Japan—Exhibitions. 2. Japan—Social life
and customs—Exhibitions. I. Brandon, Reiko Mochinaga. II.
Stephan, Barbara B. III Title: Japanese New Year.
GT4905.S65 1994   93-41794
394.2'614'0952—dc20   CIP

COVER: New Year view of the chief priest's residence, Izumo Grand Shrine
BACK COVER: Paper wand representing the spirit of fire, cut at the New Year by Kiyohara Masao, Onga Hachiman Shrine, Miyagi Prefecture
TITLE PAGE: Suwa Grand Shrine, Nagano Prefecture

CONTENTS

FOREWORD

PLANNING FOR THIS EXHIBITION and publication began approximately four years ago. The project initially focused on sacred straw ropes, *shimenawa*, but quickly grew to include all aspects of artistic creativity associated with the Japanese celebrations of the New Year, the most significant of Japan's seasonal festivals. The diverse ceremonies and activities that mark this important time provide glimpses of the religious and artistic underpinnings of Japanese society. The works of art and objects that are associated with celebration of the New Year demonstrate the creative energy, talent, and skill of untold thousands of Japanese artists. This will be the first comprehensive exhibition and the first English-language publication devoted solely to the arts and ceremonies of this significant event. Hawai'i's unique cultural diversity, including a vibrant and active Japanese-American community, makes this undertaking especially relevant for our local audience. Some aspects of the traditional Japanese New Year's celebration continue to be practiced in Hawai'i, yet much has been lost over the years or has been altered to meet the changing needs of today's people.

This traditional indigo-dyed cotton cloth, woven in Kyushu, features a delightful figure of Ebisu—one of the Seven Lucky Gods—holding a sea bream, a favorite motif of the New Year celebration. (Kitakamakura Museum.)

Change has also occurred in Japan. Contemporary Japan is a modern industrial nation, with rich and important artistic traditions that honor the past while forging new directions and forms of creative expression. Traditional aspects of celebrating the New Year remain strongest in rural areas, while rapid urbanization of much of the country has resulted in creative and pragmatic modification of traditional religious and cultural practices.

Since much of the material included in this exhibition is specifically made for the New Year and is on display for only several weeks each year, research and photography was spread over five years. Cocurators of the exhibition Reiko M. Brandon and Barbara B. Stephan made five trips to Japan during fall and winter months, braving adverse weather conditions in the country's largest cities and remote rural areas. Reiko and Barbara are responsible for both the conception and implementation of this endeavor: their scholarship, creativity, and hard work is clearly evident in every aspect of this effort. Without their dedication and commitment, this project would not have occurred.

The Academy has worked with colleagues in Japan over many years to develop programs and activities that could be presented both in Hawai'i and in Japan. Strong bonds of friendship and mutual respect have been strengthened with each passing year. Our friends in Japan have been extremely helpful, working tirelessly to assure the success of our efforts. While most of these organizations and individuals are thanked elsewhere by Ms. Brandon and Ms. Stephan, I would like to call attention to several examples of extraordinary assistance that we have received.

Our quest for a representative sample of the sacred rice-straw ropes led the curators to the Izumo Grand Shrine in Shimane Prefecture. Here Senior Priest Senge Yoshihiko made arrangements for crafting the huge *shimenawa* that is a centerpiece of the exhibition. The success of this project was due largely to the unstinting efforts of Rev. Daiya Amano and the support of the late Bishop Shigemaru Miyao of the Izumo Taisha Mission of Hawai'i. Members of the Izumo Taisha Tonbara Kannō Kōsha and the Tonbara Craft Center were responsible for creating this *shimenawa*, which will hang in front of the worship hall of the Izumo Taisha Mission of Hawai'i after the exhibition closes.

A further outstanding exhibition piece is the pair of giant *waraji* (straw sandals) created by the Waraji Preservation Society of Minami Yato in Totsuka Ward, Yokohama. Considerable time and financial resources were directed to this project, and we are most appreciative of the initiative taken by Mr. Tanaka Keishū, former member of the House of Representatives, and for the diligent efforts of Mr. Kaneko Kazuo, President of Sanpō Seiki Company, and Mr. Kaneko Tadashi, President of the Waraji Preservation Society. At the end of the exhibition the *waraji* will also find a home in Hawai'i.

Numerous other individuals and organizations in Japan made generous donations that have appreciably enriched the exhibition. A unique shrine *shimenawa* came from Chief Priest Togano Morio, Gokoku Shrine, Toyama Prefecture. Mr. Miyayama Hiromitsu of the Ishikawa Prefectural Museum of History arranged for the gift of a large Kanazawa-style rice-straw decoration. A further significant *shimenawa* was obtained through the cooperation of Mr. Nagamatsu Atsushi and the generosity of Shikaumi Jinja in Shikanoshima, Fukuoka. A collection of distinctive paper artifacts was assembled largely through the good offices of Ms. Kamekura Kakuko, a scholar who has supported the project since its inception, and Mr. Suzuki Masaka of the Miyagi Prefectural Association of Shinto Shrines, who kindly solicited the cooperation of a number of Shinto priests in his prefecture. Chief Priest Katayama Fumihiko and Secretary Mori Hisako of the Hanazono Shrine, Tokyo, provided invaluable assistance in helping us expand the exhibition collection. Mr. Sakaue Akio of Nagatoro in the Chichibu region of Saitama Prefecture kindly offered a complete set of the beautifully crafted straw and shaved-wood offerings he creates each year for the New Year and Little New Year holidays. We are greatly indebted to the generosity of these and other donors.

A number of significant exhibition pieces were loaned by the Kitakamakura Museum, through the courtesy of Ms. Kashima Kou. Shinzan Shrine and the Oga Shinzan Museum of Traditional Culture generously agreed to the loan of rare masks used in the Namahage celebration of Akita Prefecture. Important logistical assistance provided by the Azabu Museum of Arts and Crafts, Tokyo, was arranged by the museum's founder, Mr. Watanabe Kitarō. We want to thank the staff members and curators of these and the many other museums throughout Japan who provided invaluable advice and assistance.

In Honolulu the project benefited from the encouragement and support of numerous individuals and community groups. A special debt of gratitude is owed to two individuals: Mr. Walter A. Dods, Jr., Chairman and Chief Executive Officer, First Hawaiian Bank, and Mr. Yoshiharu Satoh, Chairman and Chief Executive Officer, Central Pacific Bank. They assumed a leadership role in taking the project to the community, and their efforts have been crucial to the realization of this endeavor. Mr. Kensaku Hōgen, Consul General of Japan, deserves our sincere gratitude for his enthusiastic support of this project from its inception and for his valuable guidance and assistance throughout. We would also like to recognize Mr. Clarence Lee, of Clarence Lee Design & Associates, Inc., who contributed the design for a special *ema*, or votive tablet, to commemorate the exhibition.

We are extremely grateful to the Japan Foundation Center for Global Partnership, the Japan World Exposition Commemorative Fund, the Hawaii State Foundation on Culture and the Arts, and the National Endowment for the Arts for providing major grants to this project, and to all other contributors whose support was critical to the realization of our plans. All these friends are listed elsewhere.

It is my hope that this project documenting an important aspect of traditional Japanese culture and life will lead to greater understanding and respect between all citizens of Japan and the United States.

GEORGE R. ELLIS
Director

Hagoita (battledore).

ACKNOWLEDGMENTS

THE JAPANESE NEW YEAR became a major community-oriented, multifaceted cultural event under the auspices of the Honolulu Academy of Arts only because of the contributions of numerous individuals and institutions. At the Honolulu Academy of Arts, Director George R. Ellis encouraged the broadest possible program. Susan Lampe, Director of Development, secured the funding necessary for realizing the project. Fujio Kaneko, Installations Designer, created an exceptional atmospheric installation that gave special life to the exhibit and festival. Textile Department staff members Florence Ikeda and Helen Friend, aided by volunteers Ethel Aotani, Sara Atabaki, Aki Cooke, Gail Gauldie, Sophie Hōgen, Eva Marie Judd, Muriel Smith, Jan Tagawa, and Amy Meeker, performed efficiently and with good humor the multiple tasks of preparing more than four hundred items in the exhibition. Finally, colleagues at the Academy were enthusiastic supporters of the New Year project: David J. de la Torre, Associate Director; Jim Furstenberg, Curator, Public Programs; Carol Khewhok, Curator, Academy Art Center; Kathee Hoover, Academy Shop Manager; Karen Thompson, Curator of Education; Dorothy Oshiro, Assistant Curator of Education; Stephen Little, Curator, Asian Art; Litheia Hall, Executive Secretary; Sanna Deutsch, Registrar; Jessica Rich, Public Relations Director; and Tibor Franyo, Photographer.

In Japan and Hawai'i, the Japanese New Year program has been blessed by an outpouring of support from hundreds of museums, cultural organizations, institutions, and individuals. In his Foreword, George R. Ellis, Director of the Honolulu Academy of Arts, expressed his gratitude to many who have supported this project. We would also like to acknowledge the following institutions and people whose special help has made the Japanese New Year project possible. An asterisk following a name indicates that this institution or individual was a donor to the exhibition or catalogue.

MUSEUM PERSONNEL: Fujiwara Hiroshi, Mie Prefectural Museum; Gotō Hiroshi, Fuchū City Kyōdo no Mori Museum; Hatakeyama Yutaka, Machida City Museum; Jingū Yoshihiko, Gunma Prefectural Museum of History;* Modegi Masaaki, Kite Museum; Nagamatsu Atsushi, Fukuoka City Museum;* Satō Masaya, Sendai City Museum of History and Folklore; Shigemoto Kan, Karasuyama Folk Art Museum; Sugimura Hitoshi, Mishima City Folk Museum; Takamatsu Nori, Ginza Pocket Park; Ujitani Megumi, National Museum of Ethnology; Watanabe Nobuo, Waseda University Museum of Theater; Yamaguchi Tamiya, Mitsuminesan Museum.*

OTHER ORGANIZATIONS AND INSTITUTIONS: Hawaii Okinawa Center; International House of Japan; Japan National Tourist Organization; Japan-America Society of Hawaii; Japanese Cultural Center of Hawaii; Japanese Women's Society of Honolulu; Miyata Mitsuru, Fussa City Board of Education; Nakayama Keiko, Toraya Gallery; Satō Isao, Pola Foundation for the Promotion of Japanese Culture; Shitara Atsuko, Fuchū City Education Center; Tankōsha Publishing Company; Tazu Yasuko, Gallery Muu; Machida Takashi, Urasenke Foundation of Hawaii; Yamamoto Masami, Ogano-machi Board of Education.

SHRINES AND TEMPLES: Abe Takeshi, Hakusan Shrine (Miyagi);* Gunji Mitsuho, Komine Shrine (Miyagi);* Kiyohara Masao, Onga Hachiman Shrine (Miyagi);* Kudō Sukeyoshi, Kaminoyama Hachiman Shrine (Miyagi);* Okuda Masato, Sarutahiko Shrine (Mie); Sugawara Hidehiro, Kitano Shrine (Miyagi);* Tōgō Raishun, Mōtsūji (Iwate);* United Association of Shinto Shrines (Tokyo); Yonemoto Shōjō, Naritasan Shinshōji (Chiba).

INDIVIDUALS: Arai Hideo; Banno Mieko;* James R. Brandon; Ekiguchi Kunio; Endō Chūkō;* Douglas J. C. Friend; Gōzawa Toshiyuki*; Hagiwara Hidesaburō; Hasegawa Ryōko; Hashimoto Hiroji;* Hata Ayako; Hisaki Tomoko; Honma Kazue; Isoda Hiroyasu and Mizuko; Kadoya Yasushi;* Emi Kalischer; Amy Katoh;* Kume Yasuo; Margaret Leong; Koishi Izumi; Minami Yoshikazu; Miyazawa Munetsugu and Yoshiko; Ann Nakamura; Nishikawa Katsuji;* Ōkawahara Shizuo; Onodera Masaji, Yoneko, and Atsuko; Ōshima Takehiko; Ozawa Masashi; Sakamoto Jiroku;* Sakuraba Yoshizō;* Satō Toshihiko; Terry T. Sekioka;* Suzuki Kiyoshi; Tonomura Eiichi;* Uchida Taketarō, Watanabe Mitsuomi;* Yamada Mineo; Yamada Takuei.*

And not least, we offer our most sincere bow of gratitude to those unknown Japanese craftsmen, street vendors, and participants in New Year festivities whom we were privileged to meet during the past five years. On snowy mountain roads, on rainy streets, and in sun-filled shrine grounds, they cheerfully and kindly offered their help and encouragement.

R.M.B.
B.B.S.

Gift envelope in the shape of a sea bream (*tai*), a symbol of celebration.

Note on the Japanese Calendar

I F THE JAPANESE NEW YEAR is a celebration of spring, why does it fall in the middle of winter? The answer lies in the dual calendrical system adopted from China in A.D. 604. Although usually referred to as a lunar calendar, the system actually involves both lunar and solar elements. The official or lunar calendar, used for all civil purposes, was based on the phases of the moon, with the first of each month falling at the new moon, and the full moon arriving on the fifteenth. Since twelve lunar months fall nearly two weeks short of a natural year, however, an extra (intercalary) month had to be added about once every thirty months to assure a rough correspondence between the calendar and the seasons.

Determining when to add an extra month involved coordinating the lunar system with a separate solar calendar used by farmers to calculate the appropriate time for crucial tasks such as seeding and transplanting. The solar calendar divided the natural year into twelve major and twenty-four minor units, with the latter given names of climatic or astronomical conditions ("the rains," "insects emerge from hibernation," "the winter solstice"). The calendar also recognized the four seasons of spring, summer, winter, and autumn, but interpreted their timing differently than in the West. The equinoxes and solstices that marked the beginning of the European seasons were taken as the midpoint by the Chinese, with the result that each Chinese season began six weeks earlier than its Western counterpart. Thus spring arrived on the day known in Japan as *risshun* (February 4 or 5 according to the Gregorian calendar), and the season reached its "peak of springness" at the vernal equinox forty-five days later.

The date of the lunar New Year was determined in reference to certain of the smaller divisions of the solar year. The calculation itself required a sophisticated knowledge of both lunar and solar calendars, but in general the year began at the second new moon after the winter solstice. The Gregorian date corresponding to the lunar New Year varied, but always fell between January 21 and February 19. In some years the solar marker *risshun* ("spring begins") fell before the New Year, and in other years afterwards; in either case, the two were close enough for the beginning of the lunar New Year to be looked on as the start of spring. The weather, of course, might still be cold (poets, indeed, loved to dwell on the incongruity of "spring" arriving amidst the snow), but in people's minds an important transformation had occurred: winter had been banished, and now all thoughts could focus on the stirring of life marked by the new season.

In 1873 the Meiji government abandoned the lunar

calendar and adopted the solar Gregorian system. This pushed the New Year to January 1, making the link between the celebration and the warming of spring much more tenuous than before. For years much of the population ignored the changes and continued to observe the lunar New Year, or grudgingly settled on a compromise date approximately one month later than the official holiday. Established ways died hard: as late as 1945 some 60 percent of farming communities still followed the old calendar or a modified version thereof.

Today January 1 is universally celebrated as the beginning of the year, but some of the inconsistencies engendered by the 1873 calendar change are still apparent. Numerous festivals and rituals that once occurred as part of the New Year season, for instance, now fall as late as the end of February. One of the most glaring discrepancies is Setsubun, a popular ceremony for driving out devils that occurs on the eve of *risshun*. Although once closely associated with the year-end purification rites, the observance could not be transferred to early January because of *risshun*'s fixed place (February 4 or 5) in the solar year. Today when young people throw parched beans about the house to cast out demons and call in good fortune, few have any idea they are participating in a rite of the new year.

For further information on the Japanese calendar, see Herschel Webb, "Calendar, Dates, and Time," in *Kodansha Encyclopedia of Japan* (Tokyo and New York: Kodansha International, 1983), 1:229–232; Watanabe Toshio, *Koyomi* (Calendars) (Tokyo: Kōseisha, 1937), 195–197; *Heibon daihyakka jiten* (The Heibon encyclopedia) (Tokyo: Heibonsha, 1985), 5:1126–1131, 8:1159–1160, 15:553.

Notes to the Reader

Abbreviated citations are used in the endnotes of each chapter whenever a work is cited in full in the Select Bibliography.

Japanese names are, as a rule, given in Japanese order, that is, family name followed by given name. In the case of contemporary persons, the name is given in the order preferred by the individual.

Long vowel sounds in Japanese words are indicated with a macron (as *shōgatsu*, or New Year). Following standard conventions, the macron is omitted in commonly known words and place names (for example, Shinto, Tokyo, Kyoto).

The word "shrine" refers to a Shinto place of worship; "temple" indicates a Buddhist institution.

The "beckoning cat," *maneki neko*, sits in a conspicuous position in practically every merchant's shop in Japan, gesturing customers to come inside. This smiling figure carries a large "one thousand *ryō*" gold coin, a token of prosperity in business. (Honolulu Academy of Arts, purchase, 1993.)

Opposite A *gohei*, or cut-paper wand, symbolizing the purifying spirit of fire.

Spirit
and
Symbol

THE
JAPANESE
NEW YEAR

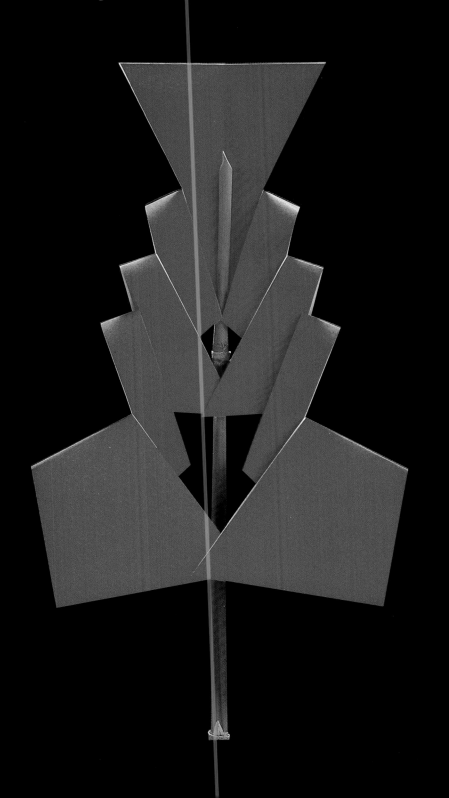

I

Spirit and Symbol

The Japanese New Year

Reiko Mochinaga Brandon

OR THE PEOPLE OF JAPAN, the New Year symbolically marks the beginning of spring, although it is celebrated in the midst of cold winter. The association of New Year with the vitality of spring derives largely from Japan's ancient agricultural tradition. New Year's greeting cards sent from snow-covered villages in northern Japan still contain the auspicious salutation *geishun*, "welcoming spring." The greeting recalls the farming cycles of planting and harvesting in which spring was seen as the inception of a bountiful year. From ancient times solar calendars adopted from China designated the midpoint between the winter solstice and the spring equinox as "the beginning of spring" (*risshun*), a period that was associated with the start of the new year. The solar New Year, or "spring new year," was once observed widely in rural Japan side by side with the government's official New Year calculated according to the phases of the moon.[1] Even when the New Year was moved to January 1 on the Gregorian calendar in the late nineteenth century, it never lost its close association with spring. New Year, or *shōgatsu*, remains the country's largest national celebration, observed everywhere through religious and civil ceremonies.

Numerous colorful festivals and ritual observances demark this rejuvenating period. They provide a special time and space in which individuals, families, and communities ready themselves for another year in the cycle of life. During my childhood in the countryside of Ibaragi Prefecture and later in the outskirts of Tokyo, I joined in, or watched my elder family members conduct, propitious New Year's activities in December and January of each year. Even in today's hectic society, deeply felt indigenous

Paper fortunes, *omikuji*, and camellia blossoms add auspicious accents of red and white to the grounds of a Shinto shrine at the New Year.

Opposite People purchase protective talismans and symbols of good fortune at shrines to place on the altar of households and businesses at the New Year. Arrows, paper wands, and exorcistic placards carry owners' prayers for protection and good fortune.

15

A pair of celebrated rocks, Meoto Iwa, "Wedded Rocks," are coastal landmarks near the imperial shrine of Ise. The rocks are likened to the god Izanagi and goddess Izanami, the mythical creators of Japan, and linked with a sacred straw rope, *shimenawa*, identifying this as a divine spot. The site is particularly dramatic at sunrise and so has become associated with the worship of the sun.

Opposite Japanese sense the divine touch of gods, *kami*, in the awesome power of nature. A gigantic cedar tree is made sacred with a sanctified rope hung with white paper streamers, *gohei*, symbols of purification.

traditions—particularly folk customs based on the Shinto religion—emerge and animate the New Year period.

New Year ceremonies and rituals pay homage to gods or deities, *kami*, who reside everywhere and control everything. In one sense, Japanese speak of the "Eight Million Gods," *yaoyorozu no kami*, as myriad. *Kami* are deities, but at the same time inhabit various earthly forms— human beings, rocks, trees, plants, and animals. The Japanese see the ultimate divine will in the rising sun; they feel sacred protection in a giant cedar tree; they sense purifying power in a gushing waterfall. Each profession and skill has its designated *kami*. *Kami* reside in the dyer's indigo vats, inhabit the carpenter's chisel, and guide the calligrapher's brush.

At the New Year season, a multitude of specific *kami* are requested to leave their sacred homes to bless the human world. New Year rituals ask the *kami* to grant worshipers assurance that the coming year will be successful and fortunate. The vast majority of deities are beneficent, but a few powerful *kami* display behavior and emotions quite like humans, including rage, jealousy, and vengefulness. In a rather intimate relationship between gods and people, these unpredictable divine souls need to be respected, worshiped, fed, talked to, and entertained. Japanese believe that a vengeful *kami*, who is tamed and

transformed through worship into a friendly protector, bestows especially effective divine benefits.

In another sense, kami is conceived to be singular, a collective entity of souls, containing all the kami we have mentioned, as well as the souls of one's dead ancestors. The soul of each deceased human, after being purified by the personal respect and worship of living relatives for a period of time, ultimately joins the universal entity of kami.[2] This conception, in spite of its vagueness, joins each person to the divine world through one's ancestors.

The Japanese call the kami who descends to revitalize the world at New Year by the fond term toshigamisama, "honorable god of the year." The concept of toshigami originates both in Chinese yin-yang cosmology with the god Harisaijo, who brings blessings from the "lucky direction," and with the Japanese god of rice, Uka no Mitama, who is welcomed at the beginning of spring. In time, the year-god also came to be identified with the spirits of one's ancestors.[3] Many elderly Japanese poignantly describe New Year as the time of the kami's "yearly visit." My grandmother often told me New Year was the occasion for getting together with the lucky god and our ancestors. The aim of her family's year-end rituals was to "lure them home and keep them happy until they leave. And hope they will return next year." Although somewhat altered in contemporary practice, the fundamental function of the New Year ceremonies is to honor and receive the toshigami, who will then bring a bountiful harvest for farmers and bestow the ancestors' blessings on everyone.

Before luring the year-god to the earth, humans must cleanse themselves of all impurities. Since ancient times, rituals of purification, especially those using purifying water, have been recognized as an effective way to counter the contamination of daily life. The Kojiki (Record of Ancient Matters) and Nihon shoki (Chronicles of Japan) vividly tell how the God Izanagi, polluted by his journey through the underworld, purifies and rejuvenates himself by bathing in water.[4] By the simple human act of cleansing, the harmful pollution of the past evaporates and the earth becomes an appropriate place for welcoming kami. Places for the divine guests—altars, shrine houses, and gardens— therefore must be dusted, swept, and washed. My mother believed that the fresh soul of a kami would descend only to a clean place and only if summoned by a pure heart. So, in her household and in many others the rather mundane task of cleaning the house was transformed into a ritual called susuharai, or "sweeping off dust," that was energetically performed a few days before the new year.[5] I remember the cold, purifying fresh air and the smell of fresh straw from new tatami mats that filled the house after this annual

Above An enormous sacred rope, *shime-nawa*, fashioned in the style of the Grand Shrine of Izumo, stretches protectively before the entrance to the main worship hall of Suwa Grand Shrine, Nagano Prefecture.

Right On New Year's morning colorfully clad worshipers purify their hands with fresh water in a cistern before approaching the sacred inner court of Heian Shrine, Kyoto. Young women, who rarely wear traditional costumes otherwise, dress in elegant kimono to match the bright spirit of the New Year.

Opposite top The old year ends with the sound of bells tolling 108 times at Buddhist temples. In Buddhist belief, the tolling symbolizes the quelling of man's 108 evil passions. At midnight a group of monks strikes the gigantic bell of Chion Temple in Kyoto.

Opposite below The year-end cleaning, *susuharai*, is obligatory preparation for the New Year and is closely associated with purification rituals. Homes, offices, stores, temples, and shrines are thoroughly cleaned and purified so that the "god of the year," *toshigami*, can descend with his blessings. Two women clean the veranda of the thatched-roof shrine in Itoigawa, Niigata Prefecture, just before the New Year.

cleaning. Shining windows and new pure-white paper in the shoji screens created a festive atmosphere, anticipating the passage from old to new that the holiday signified.

Different types of brooms made in various regions of Japan are specifically intended for the year-end cleaning. These brooms are believed to possess exorcistic power and, after being used, may be dedicated to the gods. In Fukuoka Prefecture in Kyushu, a sacred straw offering made in a shape of a small broom, called *susumite*, is placed at the altar of the kitchen deity (*kōjin*) symbolizing the ritual cleaning of his domain.[6]

Before the new year can be welcomed, a cleansing of the spirit is also required: all debts should be paid and unsettled affairs resolved. Physically and spiritually the people try to eradicate the residue of the old year so that they are ready to start anew.

As the New Year approaches, unique religious markers, offerings, and imaginative traditional decorations are installed in towns and villages throughout Japan. They demark the paths and places in front of people's houses, in shops and offices, and at roadside shrines that have been cleansed for the approaching *toshigami*. Sacred objects made with simple natural materials—freshly cut leaves of evergreen trees, entwined rice straw, and meticulously folded white paper—both designate and purify the divine areas

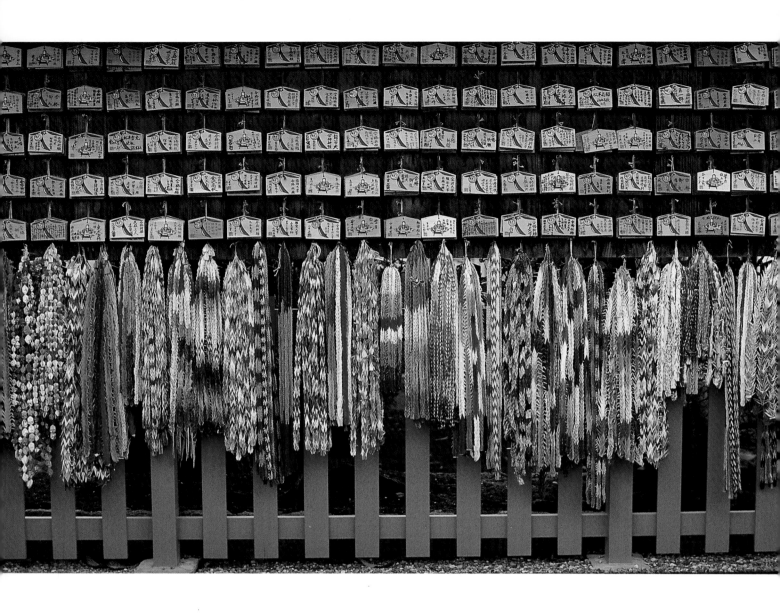

Thousands of small wooden votive tablets, *ema*, written mostly by schoolchildren asking for success in entrance examinations, petition the god of learning at Azumamaro Shrine in Kyoto. Each of the colorful folded-paper offerings on the strands of "thousand cranes," *senbazuru*, signify petitions for protection and assistance.

A young couple reads fortune papers, *omikuji*, which are sold at shrines during the New Year. Other papers have been tied like white flowers to the wooden railing. It is a popular custom to affix *omikuji* to railings, statues, doors, trees, bushes, and other accessible places in the shrine area.

and their boundaries. Auspicious *kadomatsu*, "gate pines," are placed at the entrance of people's houses and public offices to welcome the year-god. Stalks of young rice plants harvested in the early fall are plied, entwined, braided, twisted, and tied into a variety of straw forms. Straw *shimenawa*, "enclosing ropes," are hung at gates and altars, guest rooms, kitchens and other places associated with the visits of the *kami*. Sacred *gohei*, "honorable paper wand," or *yorishiro*, the god's "arrival place," made of white paper, cut and folded into crisp designs, grace sacred areas awaiting the *toshigami* to descend. In my grandmother's dark kitchen, a simple white *yorishiro* supported on a bamboo pole reflected the glow of the flame below, as if it were assuring us of the presence of something pure and new. Fire itself is sacred, providing life-sustaining heat and light to people, but its fury, while capable of devouring evil, could also bring danger. We both honored and appeased its *kami* through the *yorishiro* above the hearth.

In the final days of the year, a lively, even frantic, mood envelopes towns and villages. Shops turn into colorful year-end markets and special vendor's stalls are set up at street corners. Sellers compete loudly, calling out prices, and boasting of the quality of their special New Year merchandise. Stands are piled high with felicitous decorations, offerings, good-luck toys, vegetables, fruits, and

fish. In this vibrant, bustling market environment, food booths are always the most colorful scene, crowded with men and women shopping for the New Year feast. Preparing food for the New Year is one of the New Year's most poignant and intimate acts in households throughout Japan and was an important ritual in my grandmother's house. The sacred meal was meant for the *kami* as well as family members, and through the human act of sharing food at her dining table, these unseen, abstract sacred souls seemed to become familiar and friendly.

Rice, millet, beans, fresh vegetables, fruits, and fish—called treasures of the mountain and treasures of the sea (*yama no sachi* and *umi no sachi*)—are staples in New Year cooking. Rice, historically Japan's most important agricultural crop and the people's basic food, is an essential offering in rituals. Introduced from India via China more than two thousand years ago, rice cultivation spread to most parts of Japan by the Yayoi period (200 B.C.–A.D. 300), but until the nineteenth century rice was difficult to grow and remained scarce, making it a precious offering to the gods. Uncooked rice grains may be directly dedicated to the *toshigami* in appreciation of the harvest, along with other raw grains and fresh vegetables. The most common rice offering and food at the New Year season is *mochi*, a cooked glutinous rice cake. As early as the tenth century, various

A pair of gate pines, *kadomatsu*, marks the entrance to a traditional clothing store in Nishijin, Kyoto's traditional weaving district. Bold characters dyed on the white entrance curtain read, Obiya, "kimono sash shop," identifying the store's specialty.

kinds of *mochi* were already in use as imperial offerings at religious ceremonies.[7]

Pounding the steamed rice (*mochitsuki*) to make the smooth, sticky paste is itself a ritual. It was an inviolable year-end observance in the household of my grandmother, the matriarch of a large farming family in the Yuki district of Ibaragi Prefecture. Each year, a few days before the New Year on a "lucky" day determined by yin-yang cosmology, the whole family as well as neighborhood helpers gathered in her backyard. Hot and steaming rice from her paddy fields was placed in a large wooden mortar. Three or four young men pounded the cooked rice in a regular rhythm with heavy wooden pestles. Women reached in and skillfully flipped over the sticky mass between beats, as the rice gradually thickened into even-textured *mochi*. The special "thunk-thunk" sound of pounding *mochi*, mixed with encouraging cheers from onlookers, traveled through the village streets like footsteps of approaching good luck. The freshly pounded, extremely elastic *mochi* was rolled and formed into hundreds of round balls. Round *mochi* are especially important for, in some interpretations, they represent the god's soul.[8] My grandmother first offered two cakes of the fresh *mochi* at a special altar that had been hung in the kitchen in the proper direction for the *toshigami* to approach.[9] Then she distributed perhaps half of the *mochi*

23 ❀

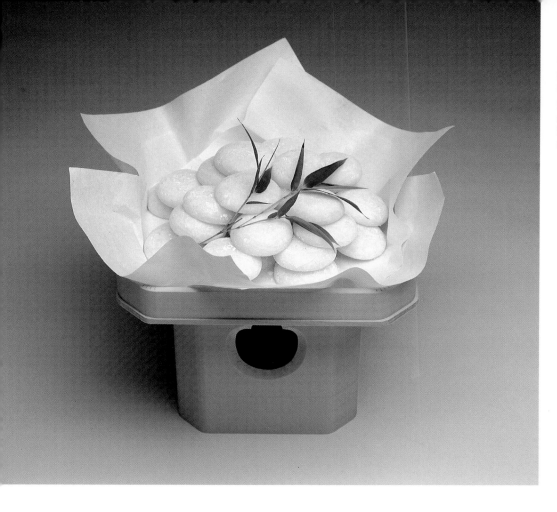

Pounded rice cakes, *mochi*, presented on a wooden tray symbolize unpretentious prayers for good fortune and good harvest. A branch of bamboo, an auspicious symbol of resilience, graces the offering.

A simple arrangement of uncooked rice and beans follows the ancient custom in agricultural Japan of presenting a token of the new harvest of "Five Grains" to the New Year god. It offers thanks for past good harvests and prayers for a bountiful coming year.

Opposite A "happiness tree," *saiwaigi*, from the remote islands of the Goto Archipelago, west of Kyushu, is hung with poignant images of a bountiful harvest: twelve straw ropes representing the months of the year, four plump radishes, a pair of sea bream, a bright longevity orange, evergreen ferns, and strips of dried seaweed. A hoe at each end of the pole celebrates the farmer's labor and skill. Mirror cakes, an orange, a pair of crossed wooden pestles, and a winnowing basket are arranged below on a wooden mortar, all auspicious New Year objects. The offered food is customarily cooked and eaten by the family during the New Year feast.

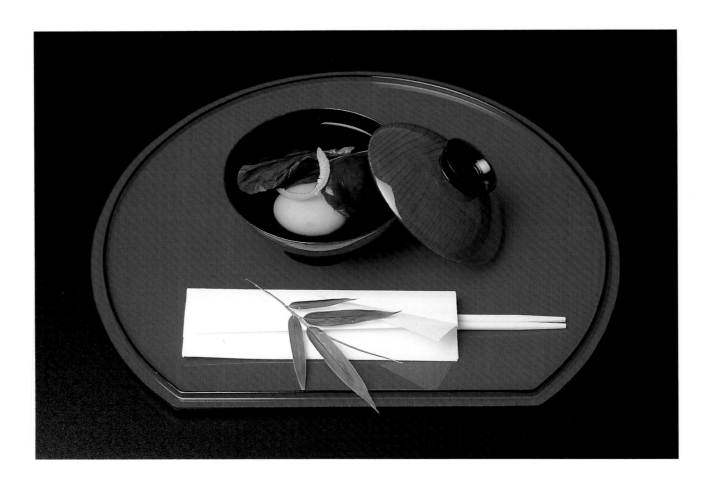

Above One food almost invariably served at the New Year breakfast is *zōni*, a hot vegetable broth that always contains one or more pieces of *mochi*, rice cake.

Imitation mirror rice cakes, made of plastic, are now available for New Year displays. The plastic forms are sold with a token offering of rice grains that can be placed inside the rice cake's hollow center.

Two men pound cooked rice in a wooden mortar to make New Year rice cakes. As one man pounds, the other flips the thickening *mochi*. The delicacy is an appropriate sacred offering at New Year: its elasticity represents strength and longevity; its white color suggests purity.

made that afternoon to relatives, helpers, and friends, as a token of the *kami*'s greetings for the coming year. Surrounded by piles of *mochi* balls and cakes, Grandmother beamed in a mood of prosperity and unfailingly announced, "With this, we can receive *toshigamisama* again." We felt genuine pleasure knowing our household would have a successful new year. My grandmother observed this custom until her death in 1950.

Kagami mochi, or "mirror rice cakes," are the most popular, and certainly the most significant, of the various auspicious foods that are dedicated to *kami* at the New Year. The origin of *kagami mochi* goes back to an imperial court ritual called *hagatame*, "teeth strengthening," first mentioned in *The Tale of Genji*.[10] Strong teeth implied good health, so an offering of large, firm rice cakes, which require sturdy teeth to eat, represented a request to the *toshigami* for many years of healthy life. The distinctive rounded-disk shape of these offertory *mochi* resembles the shape of a traditional Japanese mirror, *kagami*, hence the name. Since prehistoric times, the mirror has represented the supreme Shinto deity, Amaterasu the Sun Goddess, and the mirror has been, with the sword and the jewel, one of the three Imperial Regalia.

Mirror rice cakes may be offered wherever the *toshigami* is expected to visit. In individual households, they are most commonly placed in the *tokonoma*, the raised alcove of the guest room. During the Edo Shogunate (1600–1868), the custom of placing *kagami mochi* in the *tokonoma* was formalized in samurai households into a New Year ritual. This practice spread through Japanese society and today most families think of mirror rice cakes as their central offering to the year-god.

A *kagami mochi* is made of two stacked, flattened balls of *mochi* and is customarily placed on a small, raised wooden tray together with various good-luck emblems. A sheet of white paper, a symbol of purity, is laid under the rice cakes. Sprigs taken from evergreen plants decorate the sides: *urajiro*, whose leaves grow only in pairs, suggest longevity and the marriage bond, and *yuzuriha*, whose thick round green leaves fall only after new leaves grow, symbolize the fruitful passing of the generations from parents to children. A single bitter orange placed on top signifies longevity in two ways: its name, *daidai*, means "generation to generation"; and this fruit, while on the tree, has the unusual property of alternating between a ripe (aged) and green (youthful) condition for several years. Large pieces of seaweed are hung at the front, a further sign of longevity and of fertility. This arrangement of *mochi*, crisp white paper, delicate green plants, black seaweed, and shining bright orange creates a serene and powerful image of

Opposite On the hearth of a traditional farm kitchen, purifying oil-wick flames encircle large mirror rice cakes, *kagami mochi*. The accompanying dried seaweed, orange, and persimmons are symbols of longevity.

Left This rare pair of lacquered rice wine servers, *chōshi*, reflects the elegance of special ceremonial tableware that was used at New Year feasts in the Kanazawa area. These servers, decorated with delicate bamboo patterns, were made in the nineteenth century in Toyama Prefecture and owned by the important Okabe family, the hereditary chief retainer of the Matsudaira clan. At the official New Year ceremony, the pouring of a medicinal rice wine, *toso*, became a formal ritual, as the wine was served by a young boy and girl especially chosen for the honor. (Kitakamakura Museum.)

Below An elegant set of five lacquered bowls and tray was used to serve New Year food in the household of the lord of the powerful Maeda clan in Kaga (Kanazawa). The set reveals the superb craftsmanship of artisans in the small town of Wajima, on the northwest coast of Japan: the deep, black surface of each bowl is decorated with a gold vine pattern and the plum crest of the Maeda clan. (Kitakamakura Museum.)

worship. In my father's house in Tokyo, a *kagami mochi* decorated like this was placed in front of his Japanese sword, a symbol of the samurai heritage of his Saga clan. This display was reminiscent of the old samurai custom— placing mirror rice cakes in front of a suit of armor at the New Year—by which warriors petitioned the gods for rejuvenated strength and victory in war and life. During the turmoil of the final years of World War II, the token offering of scarce *mochi* placed before my father's sword had an air of urgency, as if trying to reach the hands of the gods. After the war ended in 1945, we celebrated many more New Years with mirror rice cakes placed in the *tokonoma*, but the Japanese sword, our family heirloom, was never brought out again.

Preparation for the coming year reaches its climax on the 31st of December. It is an extremely busy day for everyone. Women must finish cooking special dishes for the New Year's feast that are also expected to last the family and its many guests through the first three days of the year. The final cleaning of the house—or office or store—has to be done, debris must be burned, and offerings to the *toshigami* placed properly. The chores of cooking and cleaning are traditionally the tasks of women, while other important tasks—setting out gate pines, hanging rice-straw ropes, cleansing the altar, and preparing offerings—

Opposite Single Poems by 100 Poets (*hyakunin isshu*) is a traditional card game played at New Year. A leader, choosing one card from a set of 100, reads the first three lines of a classical poem; players try to identify the last two lines of the poem from a second set of 100 cards spread out in front of them. This once extremely popular New Year's pastime gave young men and women an opportunity to learn classical poetry while socializing informally. (Honolulu Academy of Arts, bequest of John Gregg Allerton, 1991.)

Left Shell Matching (*kaiawase*) was a popular game among aristocrats in the Heian period (794–1185). A forerunner of the poem-card game, players competed to match two clamshell halves containing the complementary parts of either a painting or a classical poem. Each gold-painted shell in this elegant set, which belonged to the Abe lords of Mutsu, depicts a vignette of imperial court life, reminiscent of the twelfth-century illustrated scrolls of *The Tale of Genji*. (Honolulu Academy of Arts, gift of Mrs. Walter F. Dillingham, 1948.)

are traditionally designated to men to perform. (In the past women were considered ritually impure and so could not perform sacred activities.) In each household, the male who is called upon to perform these duties is known as "man of the year" (*toshi otoko*), usually the head-of-family or eldest son. My samurai father, who would not touch a broom otherwise, dusted our Shinto altar to prepare it each year to welcome the year-god. A large number of sacred placards dedicated to *kami*, collected over the years on visits to shrines, dwelled side by side in our simple altar: Amaterasu the Sun Goddess; Hachiman the protective deity of the Minamoto (Genji) clan, from which my father liked to say our family was descended; Inari, or Uka no Mitama no Kami, protector of rice and the five grains; Tenjin, the deification of the historical Sugawara Michizane and patron-god of learning; and more. Father carefully dusted the sacred placard (*ofuda*) of each god and purified the altar with a simple sacred rope. Then he placed a pair of evergreen *sakaki* branches and two white porcelain bottles of sake before the gods. Finally he inserted a delicate split bamboo, *miki no kuchi*, "mouth of sacred wine," into each bottle, saying this would call the year-god's attention to the sacred drink. *Sake*, made of rice, represents fertility and so it is the most appropriate drink to offer the gods. It is also an indispensable part of the New Year feast. *Sake*, my

father said, lifted people up into a world where they could meet the descending gods. This comment by a *sake*-loving individual may have been self-serving, but it nonetheless reflects the sense of sharing life with the divine spirits, which animates the Japanese New Year.

The last day of the old year ends with the tolling of a bell 108 times at every major Buddhist temple in Japan. Buddhism is mostly overshadowed by Shinto and other ethnic religious customs during New Year. But the 108 bells of New Year's Eve (*joya no kane*) dramatically proclaim the transition from old to new. Powerfully high or tenderly low, the sounds of bells from different temples intermingle and echo in the icy winter air of cities and mountain villages. Starting at midnight, each strike of the bell is made slowly and deliberately by priests and by worshipers; more than an hour later the 108th sounding of the bell slowly fades. Many believe the bell tolls the quelling of man's 108 evil passions.[11] Or it is said the bell counts the seasons and months of a year.[12] Originating in China in the Sung dynasty (960–1126), the Buddhist tolling of *joya no kane* to mark the year end was adopted in Japan by Zen temples in the Kamakura period (1185–1333). For most Japanese, listening to the tolling bell induces a moment of reflection: whether the year was good or not, it is now passing. With each reverberation, listeners hope that bad

Bright papier-mâché masks of a forest sprite (*tengu*) and a fox, popular figures of folk religion, are widely sold at city bazaars for displays at New Year. There is a sense of urban chic in the humorous face of the long-nosed forest sprite and in the crafty expression on the white-and-gold fox face. (Honolulu Academy of Arts, purchase, 1993.)

Above Newly painted *tengu* masks are lined to dry at the shop of a mask maker in Miharu, Fukushima Prefecture, north of Tokyo.

Opposite A pair of New Year chopsticks is presented within meticulously folded white paper, dressed with celebratory gold and red ties.

experiences, misbehavior, wrong deeds, and ill luck of the past year are wiped away and good fortune is ushered in with the New Year.

As one year ends with the sound of bells fading away into the dark sky over Buddhist temples, another year begins at Shinto shrines. Before dawn millions of well-wishers visit shrines to receive the *kami*'s blessing for the coming year. Nowadays the largest shrines, such as Meiji Shrine in Tokyo and the Heian Shrine in Kyoto, are inundated by human waves of worshipers. In earlier times, visits were paid to shrines located in the "good-luck direction" determined by the calendar of that particular year. People worship at the local shrine dedicated to the special protective deities of that neighborhood. Ōmiya Hachiman Shrine, where we worshiped in our neighborhood in Tokyo, was surrounded by a small forest. From midnight to the dawn of New Year, it became a bright sanctuary with burning candles and a large bonfire. Before the sun rose, my father, alone, would report the events of the past year to the gods, thank them for our good fortune while making apologies for his wrong deeds, and request the god's continued blessing. It was a ritual I knew he would perform, on behalf of our family, without fail. Along with many talismans of good luck, he brought back

a small amount of water from the well at the shrine as a symbol of purification.

It is an ancient custom to cherish water collected from a well on the first morning of the year. In yin-yang cosmology, water is one of the five indispensable elements of life: it nourishes plants, therefore giving life and youth.[13] A cistern of fresh water is provided at the entrance to each shrine to purify hands and mouth before worshiping. The water of the new year, *wakamizu*, "young water," especially banishes evil and rejuvenates the body and the soul. In the Heian period (794–1185), water taken from a well in the lucky direction was offered to the Emperor on the morning of the New Year.[14]

Families in some parts of Japan still collect "young water." In Tokyo, for many years my father, dressed in formal black kimono, performed the ritual at our small family well. My mother, brother, sister, and I silently watched him ladle the "young water" into a pristine wooden bucket purified with a *sakaki* branch. After he offered some of the water to the year-god, we used the rest of it to purify our faces and hands. In that icy cold water splashing over my face, I felt another year arrive.

Many Japanese ethnologists distinguish celebratory festival periods from ordinary times with the term *hare*, "bright" or "clear." The New Year morning in our home in Tokyo seemed illuminated by a special holiday brightness. Everyone in our extended family, wearing new or special garments, gathered in the reception room, which appeared transformed into a different and sacred space by the candles burning on the altar and the *kagami mochi* decorating the alcove. The colorful array of New Year food also distinguished our table from any other day. Most dishes were served in bright red lacquer boxes or bowls bearing such propitious patterns as cranes and turtles, pines, plums, and other images of long life. In equally bright red lacquer cups, *toso*, rice wine flavored with eight kinds of medicinal herbs, was served to toast in the New Year. *Toso* is believed to ward off illness, and so it is usually a child's first taste of alcohol. The word *toso* itself is an exorcistic incantation meaning "destroying evil." The lacquer *toso* server was garnished with red and white papers folded into a butterfly shape. Our chopsticks were wrapped in white paper tied with gold and silver strands. The color red—of blood, fire, the sun, a symbol of life—accented by shining gold and silver, dominated the table, creating an aura of bursting energy. The day's feast effectively transposed our lives from the old, subdued winter to a new, bright, and hopeful spring. As a child, I felt a magical beginning in this formal celebration of our family.

The most important New Year ritual for us children

Opposite This superbly woven resist-pattern *(kasuri)* cloth from Kyushu may have served as a decorative hanging during the holiday season. It features a display of *kagami mochi* (mirror rice cakes), the major offering of the New Year. Presented on a raised ceremonial tray, the rounded rice cakes are graced with an orange and bamboo leaves, symbols of longevity and resilience. (Kitakamakura Museum.)

At the New Year season people dress up in special garments, either new or heirlooms. This exceptional commoner's outer jacket of indigo cotton carries a design particularly appropriate for the New Year: a gigantic phoenix and, under its arching wings and tail feathers, such good-luck symbols as an invisible cape, magical hat, lucky mallet, and money bag. A large metal eye in the head of the phoenix adds mystic energy to the garment. (Honolulu Academy of Arts, purchase, 1986.)

Kites flying freely and high in the sky have long been associated with religious events in Japan. Kite-flying at New Year became widely popular during the Edo period when kites of many styles and sizes were flown, singly and in communal contests. The two priestly families of the Grand Shrine of Izumo flew kites made in the shape of the character *tsuru*, crane, to celebrate childbirth. The crane is believed to live for 1,000 years and hence is a symbol of longevity. Shown here is a contemporary version of the crane kite, which was crafted by the Takahashi family in Izumo. (Honolulu Academy of Arts, purchase, 1993.)

came after the feast, when Father took out a pile of small envelopes. Beaming with a questioning smile, he asked each of us, starting with the youngest, "Well now, what age have you become this year?" Until about fifty years ago, New Year was the time people added a year to their age. Therefore, a child, who was traditionally said to be one year old at the birth, became a year older on New Year's day. When I reported my new age to Father, I felt a little older. And when he gave me a small envelope containing cash, *toshidama*, "treasure of the year," I felt rewarded for my new maturity. For centuries in Japan, it has been a popular custom for elders and superiors to give New Year gifts to children and subordinates. The "treasure," whether money, a rice cake, or other gift, is traditionally considered a special present brought to the child by the *toshigami*. The idea remains strong that at New Year each of us receives blessings from the gods and that families celebrate another healthy year for their growing children.

From January 1st through the 3rd, the whole nation of Japan seems to pause on holiday. City streets are deserted, except around shrines and temples, offices are closed, and most shops shut their doors. The home is the center of activities and the gathering place for families. Games are brought out for children, kites decorated with

Top Akabeko, a good-luck toy made in the Aizu district of northern Japan, commemorates a legendary red cow that carried lumber to build Enzōji, an important Buddhist temple in Aizu. The papier-mâché animal is a talisman that expels disease, and so bestows good health. Its bobbing head has entertained children and adults for almost four centuries. (Honolulu Academy of Arts, purchase, 1993.)

Left Sanbasō is the auspicious dance performed at New Year in the classic Kyōgen comedy theatre. A rounded, papier-mâché figure of Sanbasō (made by Miyauchi Fusa, Takamatsu, Kagawa Prefecture) reflects Japan's unpretentious folk doll tradition. The yellow hat with the red sun, red chin cord, and yellow trousers with young pine trees are realistic details of the Sanbasō costume worn on the Kyōgen stage. (Honolulu Academy of Arts, purchase, 1993.)

Right Ebisu is a popular guardian figure, one of the Seven Lucky Gods, especially honored by merchants and fishermen at the New Year. This delightful papier-mâché figure of Ebisu (made by Hashimoto Hiroji, Miharu, Fukushima Prefecture) portrays a fat, smiling deity standing atop a huge sea bream, suggesting a bounteous and prosperous future. (Honolulu Academy of Arts, purchase, 1993.)

A fishing fleet in Mie Prefecture, central Japan, is decorated for the New Year's ceremonial "first fishing," *hatsu ryō*. A host of colorfully dyed banners and flags that fly from the ships' masts communicate the bright energy and optimism of the New Year.

Opposite Fishermen of the Boso Peninsula, south of Tokyo, wear a ceremonial outer jacket, *maiwai*, to inaugurate the New Year and assure a rich catch in the coming year. This nineteenth-century *maiwai* depicts three dancer-musicians celebrating a big catch. The central dancer is carrying a large, sacred Shinto paper wand over his shoulder and an open fan inscribed with large red characters reading, "Great Catch." (Honolulu Academy of Arts, purchase, 1984.)

auspicious warrior figures fly high in the sky, and century-old battledores (*hagoita*) are displayed for their propitious decorations (if not actually used to play shuttlecock). Cheerful, often humorous, folk toys and good-luck objects decorate home altars, shelves, and walls. Their lively images—seven lucky gods, treasure ships, twelve zodiac animals, good-luck cat, money-collecting rakes, *daruma* dolls, and gold coins—assure the presence of good fortune. As a child I thought this playful and joyous period was filled with all the good luck in the world.

Every activity has its ceremonial start at the New Year, with the word "first" (*hatsu*) attached to it—the first sunrise (*hatsu hinode*), first dream (*hatsu yume*), first tea ceremony (*hatsu gama*), first fish catch (*hatsu ryō*). People pay particular attention to the first sunrise, for this is the sacred marking of the first day of the New Year. In olden times, it was believed that placing a picture of a lucky treasure ship under your pillow would bring a lucky first dream and good fortune for the rest of the year. One's best effort was required on any "first" occasion in order to ensure success throughout the coming year. I remember that when I wrote my "first calligraphy" of the year, I tried to make my brush marks strong to assure progress in writing skill during the year. The first business transaction or the first office work of the year is likewise treated with ceremony,

The tiger is one of the twelve zodiac animals in yin-yang cosmology, conveying in Japan an image of bravery, power, and judicial awe. Perhaps because the animal is not indigenous and hence not feared, the tiger is represented in popular culture as a protective amulet or a friendly child's toy. The tail of this bright yellow papier-mâché tiger (from Miharu, Fukushima Prefecture) snaps with vitality; its fierce expression is belied by a touch of humor in the eyes and mouth. (Honolulu Academy of Arts, purchase, 1993.)

Opposite This beautiful mid nineteenth-century lion head with gold eyes and teeth once belonged to the Maeda samurai family of Ishikawa Prefecture. Such finely crafted red-and-black lacquerwear lion heads are cherished as sophisticated "good fortune objects," *engimono*, of the New Year, displayed in homes to bring good fortune and ward off harmful spirits. (Kitakamakura Museum.)

especially at large firms, banks, and retail businesses.

At shrines and temples, ritual dances and plays performed at New Year bring the *kami* into the public sphere. *Kagura*, the most ancient performances in Japan, present lively portrayals of gods who bestow good fortune and expel evil. *Kagura*, literally "god pleasure," are Shinto dances whose origins lie in the mythical dance that Ame no Uzume performed to lure Amaterasu the Sun Goddess out of a cave to which she had withdrawn in anger, plunging the world into darkness. Amaterasu emerges from the cave to watch Ame no Uzume's felicitous *kagura* dance, thus restoring light, and spring, to the world.[15] This story is replicated in New Year rituals: the *toshigami* is enticed to join the world of humans through offerings, including dance and song. In hundreds of local forms of sung or danced *kagura*, the *kami* are entertained or are impersonated by village dancers in order to seek the rejuvenation of the world and banish the dark, god-less winter.

The performance most closely enacting the ancient Amaterasu legend is known as Iwato Kagura, "Kagura of the Cave." Masked performers in the Takachiho district of Kyushu, the sacred place where the ancient Shinto gods are said to have descended to earth, joyously enact the gods dancing before Amaterasu's sacred cave to the accompaniment of drums and flutes. Iwato Kagura is often a spectacu-

lar public performance, danced on a high stage before a large audience.

Other festival *kagura* dances are performed in intimate, even conversational, circumstances. In the Boiling Water (*yudate*) Kagura of the Kitashitara district of Aichi Prefecture, propitiated demons use their fierce energy to suppress evil spirits. The demons dance and converse with spectators gathered at a farmhouse designated for the festival, thereby intermingling the sacred world of the *kami* with the human world of the village. During the festival performance, sacred water is boiled in a large vat and then sprinkled on all the participants and spectators, purifying the space, the demons, and people living in the village alike. Villagers also call it the Flower Festival, *hana matsuri*, thus magically invoking the spring season.[16]

A very special *kagura* dance, *shishi mai*, the lion dance, brings New Year's blessings into private homes. The lion dance originated in Tang-dynasty China and was brought to Japan as one of many Buddhist and court dances in medieval times. The one-man and two-man lion dances seen in Kanto and Kansai at the New Year are offshoots of *kagura* long associated with the Ise Shrine and the Atsuta Shrine that bring the god's presence to people unable to visit a shrine at New Year.[17] I remember the *shishi*'s large wooden head and green body energetically cavorting in and out of house gates, jaws snapping and feet stamping to drum and flute music. People, believing that the *shishi* can cure illness and disease, placed money on their shoulders or heads as a token of appreciation. As the dancing lion swallowed the money with its large mouth, it touched the ailing spectator and conferred the god's power.

After the official three-day celebration of the holiday, the atmosphere of New Year gradually changes. Between the 3rd and 5th of January, stores and shops reopen, bearing banners and signs that announce the first sale of the year. Shrines and temples are busy, as throngs of worshipers continue to pay their respects, but now the country begins to return to its ordinary schedule with new energy. Office workers return to their jobs cherishing new ambitions and housewives undertake their daily chores in a rejuvenated spirit. Decorations marking the new year begin to disappear from streets and homes. Mirror rice cakes are removed from sacred places and are cooked into various dishes; families share this final meal with the gods to celebrate the final phase of the New Year. Around the 7th of January, gate pines and sacred straw ropes are taken down from entrances and gateways. It is the time for the *toshigami* to return to their divine homes. Around the 15th of January, these discarded pines and ropes are burned to facilitate the god's departure and expel harmful spirits

Right A powerful demon, *oni*, quells evil and brings protection at the Flower Festival in Aichi Prefecture. The demon's supernatural strength is shown by the fierce mask and gigantic ax. Bamboo poles festooned with paper streamers demark the sacred performance area, in which a musician wearing a festival jacket beats a large drum to accompany the dancing and posturing.

Below The mask of the beneficent lion, *shishi*, is worn by a skilled performer in the lion dance. This exorcistic dance is believed to banish evil and bestow the god's blessings when performed at New Year. Originating in China, the lion dance is related to sacred *kagura* dances of the imperial shrine of Ise.

from the area, a practice recorded as early as the Heian period.[18] Today, the rising flame of a ritual bonfire, often reaching fifteen feet in the air, draws a communal gathering that includes many children. My grandmother said the fire was "a farewell to the god-spirits" who were leaving behind an abundance of fresh energy for us.

New Year in Japan embraces, like yin and yang, two contrasting and complementary characteristics, making the season complex and fascinating. New Year is a religious holiday replete with numerous ritual observances. It is a quiet and intimate period for families, who become united at this time. It is a time for personal self-examination, for sincere introspection into one's behavior. Time slows and the energy of life focuses inward, bringing spiritual cleansing. The intimate and serene quality of the New Year is reflected in its religious objects. The cut and folded forms of white paper demonstrate the beauty of simplicity and symbolize quiet purity. The simple materials, laboriously transformed into various sacred articles, express an intimate form of worship. The colors of nature and the pure forms of the objects used to observe the religious New Year are deep expressions of a Japanese esthetic of simplicity and reverence.

The other face of the Japanese New Year is lively and active, a fast-moving, fun-filled, bursting-with-energy festival. People perceive the world as packed with all kinds of "good fortune," which they want to invite into their lives and homes. Troubles are set aside and only a bright future is contemplated during this time. New Year erupts with optimistic, outgoing energy that spills out in all directions and for everyone. Lively ritual *kagura* performances attract audiences to shrines, theaters, and street corners. Outdoor competitions, games, kite-flying, and firemen's acrobatic demonstrations enliven public places. The special openness of the season may prompt normally reserved Japanese to exchange greetings for a bright New Year with strangers in the street. The linking of New Year with the fecundity of spring is seen in bright-colored good-luck decorations and charms, in richly painted kites and New Year's toys, and in children's games that bring gaiety and joy. Otherwise peaceful shrine halls of worship are encircled at the New Year season by a warren of jam-packed vendors' stalls. Shouting pitchmen hawk snacks, drinks, gaudy souvenirs, and bright and colorful trinkets, charms, and amulets. The primary colors and vibrant shapes of this aspect of the New Year represent another Japanese aesthetic, which seeks to find a balanced beauty from multiplicity, variety, and above all, exuberant energy. When Japanese observe the New Year season, they celebrate both the serene and religious, the energetic and

Okina is a unique ritual dance-drama performed at Shinto shrines and Noh stages during the New Year. When the actor dons the serene white mask of the god Okina, "old man," he is possessed by and becomes the god. At Yasaka Shrine in Kyoto, the god's dance, *kami gaku*, bestows Okina's blessings for a long life.

hedonistic, for these are understood to be two necessary, coexisting aspects of human life.

Today Japanese live in a society that welcomes technological change even when it occurs at perplexing speed. Old communal and religious ties stubbornly endure alongside contemporary fast food, rock music, video games, and honeymoons in Hawai'i. On reflection, it would seem that as a result of Japanese religion's flexibility, new and old ideas are able to share the same space, and time is not linear but interpenetrating and overlapping: a vacuum cleaner helps the New Year sweeping, a white paper *gohei* blesses the gas stove, a pine sprig hangs from the radiator of a firetruck, a computerized machine churns out *mochi*. A young man in blue jeans and punk haircut visits Meiji Shrine with his kimono-clad girlfriend. There is a moment when he and she both accept the *toshigami*'s blessing that lives in the white arrow purchased at the inner shrine. Perhaps two of three Japanese today visit a shrine at New Year, suggesting the tenacious hold of traditional ways. As long as Japanese people believe that *kami* protect and nourish their land and their families, celebration of the New Year will continue to be the major festive event in the year.

NOTES

1. See Note on the Japanese Calendar, p. 11.

2. Miyake Hitoshi, *Seikatsu no naka no shūkyō*, 35.

3. The "goddess of the lucky direction," is mentioned in Abe Haruaki's *Hokinaiden*, 1209. Yin-yang cosmology identifies a "lucky direction" for each year, determined by locating where the year occurs within a diagram that relates the four cardinal directions, the twelve zodiac animals, and the ten-day cycle, the latter a combination of light-dark (yin-yang) and the five elements. The *Kojiki* (Record of Ancient Matters) contains the story of Uka no Mitama, the god of rice and grains. In archaic Japanese, the word *toshi* meant both "year" and "rice" or "harvest." See also Kadokawa Shoten, ed., *Zusetstu haiku daisaijiki*, 5:293, and Yoshino Hiroko, *Onyō gogyō to Nippon no minzoku*, 25–62.

4. Donald Philippi, ed. and trans., *Kojiki* (Princeton, NJ, and Tokyo: Princeton University Press and Tokyo University Press, 1969), 61–70.

5. Some people observe the ritual cleaning on December 13, the date Edo Castle was cleaned during the Edo period (1600-1868). Suzuki, *Nihon nenchū gyōji jiten*, 673.

6. Suzuki, *Nihon nenchū gyōji jiten*, 674.

7. Offerings of *mochi* are mentioned in *Engi-shiki* (Procedures of the Engi Era), compiled by Fujiwara Tokihira and others, a description of ceremonies and etiquette of the Heian period. Shinmura Izuru, *Kōjien* (Tokyo: Iwanami Shoten, 1955), 242.

8. Origuchi, *Nenchū gyōji*, in *Origuchi Shinobu zenshū*, 15:104–105.

9. The year-god may be welcomed at the permanent family altar. But because the god comes from the "lucky direction" of the year, often a special "altar of the lucky direction" (*ehōdana*) was built to welcome the year-god.

10. Murasaki Shikibu, *Genji monogatari* (The tale of Genji), vol. 2, in *Nihon koten bungaku taikei* (Complete collection of classical Japanese literature), Takagi Ichinosuke et al., ed. (Tokyo: Iwanami Shoten, 1959), 15:377.

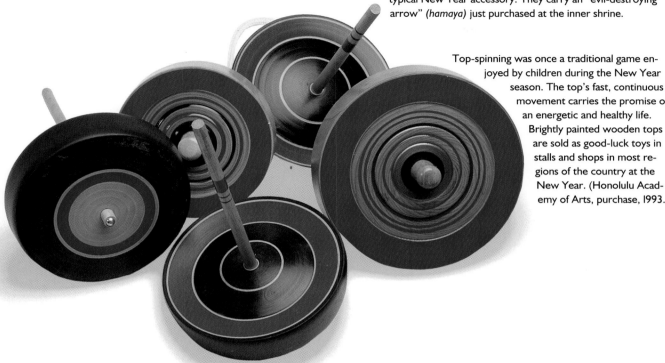

Opposite A young man casually dressed in jeans, boots, plaid shirt, and visor cap visits Meiji Shrine in Tokyo on the 3rd day of January with his kimono-clad girl friend, whose white boa is a typical New Year accessory. They carry an "evil-destroying arrow" *(hamaya)* just purchased at the inner shrine.

Top-spinning was once a traditional game enjoyed by children during the New Year season. The top's fast, continuous movement carries the promise of an energetic and healthy life. Brightly painted wooden tops are sold as good-luck toys in stalls and shops in most regions of the country at the New Year. (Honolulu Academy of Arts, purchase, 1993.)

11. The figure 108 is arrived at by adding the product of six sense roots (eyes, ears, nose, tongue, body, and emotion) times three movements (pain, pleasure, and avoidance) to the product of six sense roots times three feelings (liking, disliking, and fear), then mutiplying by three durations (past, present, and future).

12. Adding together 12 months, 24 half-months (*sekki*), and 72 three-part divisions (*kō*) of each *sekki* equals 108.

13. In yin-yang theory, the five elements exist in positive and negative relationships. The positive, yang, relations are: wood makes fire, fire produces earth, earth creates metal, metal makes water, and water grows wood. The negative, yin, relations are: water smothers fire, fire melts metal, metal cuts wood, wood (tree) penetrates earth, and earth dams water. In the fixed universe of yin-yang, New Year is designated as the time of wood, its season is spring, and its color is green. See Yoshino Hiroko, *Onyō gogyō*, 26–31.

14. Suzuki, *Nihon nenchū gyōji jiten*, 52–4.

15. Philippi, *Kojiki*, 81.

16. Haga Hideo, "Hanamatsuri no sato" (Home of the flower festival), in *Matsuri* (Festival), vol. 6, in *Nihon hakken* (Discover Japan) (Tokyo: Akatsuki Kyōiku Tosho, 1979), 43–50.

17. Kawatake Toshio, ed., *Engeki hyakka daijiten* (Encyclopedia of theater), vol. 3 (Tokyo: Heibonsha, 1960), 82.

18. Suzuki, *Nihon nenchū gyōji jiten*, 219–228.

II
Sacred Symbols
The Decorations of the New Year

Barbara B. Stephan

AS THE YEAR DRAWS TO A CLOSE in Japan, street markets spring to life and temporary stalls crop up on neighborhood corners. Here—amidst the rice cakes, candies, and other year-end delicacies—the decorations that play a central role in the New Year celebration can be found. They are objects of simple beauty, made from materials of little intrinsic value: straw, pine branches, paper, unvarnished wood, and bamboo. Once in their designated places—framing the entryway and adorning the altar or alcove inside the home—they set the stage for the festive period ahead.

The New Year's decorations as a group are often referred to by the special name *okazari*. The base word, *kazari*, means nothing more than decoration in a purely secular sense; it is the honorific "o" that sets these objects apart and hints at their sacred function. For all New Year decorations have a single purpose: to prepare a seat where the deity bringing the blessings of the New Year, *toshigami*, can be welcomed and entertained. In practice the sacred symbolism of the holiday decorations is often taken for granted, and few people spend time pondering the nature of the year-god or the specific function of individual ornaments. Instead the decorations are put up out of custom and enjoyed for their beauty and the distinctive flavor they lend to the season.

Detail of a massive rice-straw *shimenawa* found at Izumo Grand Shrine in western Japan.

Opposite A thatched-roof farmhouse is seen through the *torii* (entry gate) of a small local shrine in the Hida region of Gifu Prefecture. The rice-straw rope, freshly hung at the New Year, will stay in place until the end of the year.

Sometime in the Edo period *shimenawa* developed into a variety of elaborate and decorative shapes. Japan's most famous and impressive sacred rope is found at Izumo Grand Shrine in Shimane Prefecture. This smaller version of the main shrine's massive *shimenawa* hangs in front of the residence of the chief priest. Few craftsmen possess the technical skill necessary to create this dynamic sculptural form.

Although it may appear that the spiritual content of the holiday symbols has been obscured, religious concepts still frame people's behavior. Most households undertake a vigorous housecleaning before putting up the decorations, which is a secular equivalent to the purification rituals required in Shinto before greeting the gods. Families that have experienced a death during the year generally forego the New Year display entirely, a gesture influenced by the Shinto belief that death is an impurity the gods shun.[1] Traditional concepts of purity and pollution also underlie the insistence on decorating only with items that are new and fresh, such as crisp white paper or straw and bamboo still tinged with green.

New Year decorations are categorized as *engimono*, things that bring luck. Because the good fortune they promise derives from some higher power, the objects are treated with decorum. When purchasing the decorations, it is considered unseemly to haggle over price as one might for other items sold in street markets, and a buyer who tries may be gently rebuked with the admonition "after all, it's an *engimono*, it belongs to the gods." After being displayed in places of honor for the duration of the holiday, the decorations are never simply discarded, but are instead taken down and set aside for ritual burning, often on the grounds of a nearby shrine.

Good-luck charms are particularly valued by those in high-risk occupations, to whom skipping the New Year's display would be tantamount to inviting misfortune. A construction site or a shipyard without a simple pine or straw ornament standing guard during the holiday is almost unthinkable. Pinball parlors—where luck is the players' most cherished companion—often sport the most lavish displays of all.

In the past when villagers craved time off, they reportedly slipped a pine arrangement in front of the headman's house. Regardless of the season, he was sure to take the hint and announce a "New Year" break.[2] While this practice has lapsed, the purpose of the decorations remains the same: to herald the holiday and invite renewal.

Shimenawa: SACRED ROPES OF STRAW

The *shimenawa*, or sacred straw rope, is the most distinctive of the festive ornaments of the New Year season. It is also one of the most ancient, having roots in the indigenous faith that became the foundation for Shinto. The *shimenawa* serves as a ritual marker separating the realm of the sacred from that of the profane. Contrary to the customary practice of rope-making, the strands of rice straw that make up the *shimenawa* are twisted to the left rather than to the right. This ritual inversion, a magical practice associated in numerous cultures with such taboos as death and pollution, imbues the rope with mystical power.

Shimenawa are not limited in use to the New Year. Hanging from the *torii* (entrance gateway) or in front of the worship hall, the sacred ropes are one of the classic markers of a Shinto shrine. When used to encircle large trees or stones, they announce the sacred presence thought to pervade these natural objects. Whether surrounding a festival float or (in a cloth version) girdling the waist of a sumo champion, the left-twisted rope separates the world of the pure from the impure.

In addition to demarcating sacred space, *shimenawa* have from ancient times functioned as devices to repel malevolent spirits. Picture scrolls of the Kamakura period (1185–1333) show that it was once common practice to stretch a straw rope hung with protective herbs or a wooden talisman between the gate posts at the entrance to a dwelling. Boundary ropes also marked the road leading into a village. Decorated with magical charms or phallic images, they announced the power of the local deity and challenged harmful spirits to keep their distance.[3]

Tradition dates the use of *shimenawa* back to mythological time, citing the famous tale of the Sun Goddess Amaterasu as recorded in Japan's earliest chronicles, the *Kojiki* (Record of Ancient Matters, A.D. 712) and the *Nihon*

shoki (Chronicles of Japan, A.D. 720). Offended by the defiling behavior of her unruly brother, the Sun Goddess hid in a cave, plunging the world into darkness. The deities schemed to lure the reluctant goddess out, then stretched a twisted rice-straw rope behind her to block her retreat. The myth has been interpreted as a symbolic enactment of the death and rebirth of the sun, which parallels the regeneration of the seasons in spring.[4]

Although most Japanese consider the shimenawa a native tradition, the custom is hardly unique to the archipelago. Ropes similar in function are found in China, Southeast Asia, and as far west as India and Nepal, leading some scholars to suggest that the practice originated on the Asian continent. Others look to South Pacific funeral customs, in which a left-twisted rope is used to symbolize the division between the world of the living and that of the dead. Whatever its origin, most agree that the shimenawa was ultimately transmitted to Japan via Korea, the country where the closest parallels to Japanese usage are found. Although no longer common in Korea, the sacred marker once was hung in front of the homes of newborns, above the gate at the New Year, and at the entrance to the shrine erected for the festival of the community god.[5]

Originally a ritual divider, the left-twisted rope

with its magical properties eventually came to be associated with the New Year in Japan. Some scholars credit Chinese influence, citing records describing the sixth-century Chinese New Year practice of hanging a bulrush rope above the doorway to dispel pestilence.[6] Not until 935, however, can a similar custom be documented in Japan. In that year the poet and diarist Ki no Tsurayuki passed New Year's day far from the imperial capital of Kyoto, and his diary expresses his wistful longing for home: "I can't help thinking about the capital today. I wonder how it all looks—the straw festoons. . . at the gates of the little houses."[7]

Tsurayuki's mention of "little houses" hints that the New Year's tradition of hanging shimenawa was a folk practice, rather than one that had spread from the aristocracy. This observation is born out by a twelfth-century scroll painting, the Annual Rites and Ceremonies (Nenchū gyōji emaki), which offers the first glimpse of seasonal practices. While the New Year segments focus on formal court ceremonies adopted from China, one small scene—a view of commoners peering out of their modest row houses to watch an imperial procession—gives a clue to popular practice. Here, barely visible in front of each doorway, is a slender rope, hung intermittently with strips of paper or hemp and the leaves of what appears to be the yuzuriha tree.[8]

Sometime between the twelfth and seventeenth centuries the simple straw rope that had begun as a rustic gesture to welcome the New Year deity and ward off misfortune underwent a metamorphosis. The modest single strand spawned countless regional variations, many elaborate and highly decorative. Sadly, however, few writers or painters considered the straw ornaments worthy of documentation, and since *shimenawa* are customarily burnt after use, little remains to chronicle the process of transformation.

The era of peace and prosperity that began in the Edo period (1600–1868) brought many changes, among which was a renewed interest in seasonal customs and observances. Woodblock prints and written commentaries indicate that by the end of the seventeenth century many variations of *shimenawa* existed. Feudal lords, required by law to maintain a residence in the new capital of Edo (Tokyo), brought with them their native styles and vied with one another for the most impressive effect. Between tall poles of pine and bamboo Lord Nabeshima of Saga suspended a huge hourglass-shaped straw drum that was decorated with lobster and bright orange citrus. In front of the Nambu mansion hung two large salted sea bream, along with lobster, various types of dried seaweed, and other ornaments with auspicious associations. At the Lord

Opposite A priest at Fushimi Inari Shrine in Kyoto blesses the New Year's *shimenawa* before it is hung in front of the worship hall.

Above left A unique *shimenawa* in the shape of a hand drum is suspended at the entry to Yoga Shrine in Saga City (Kyushu). A similar shape once hung in front of the Saga lord's mansion in the capital of Edo (Tokyo), exciting the comment of contemporary observers.

Above right The mature rice grains hanging from the sacred rope at Fushimi Inari Shrine honor the shrine's patron deity, the god of rice production.

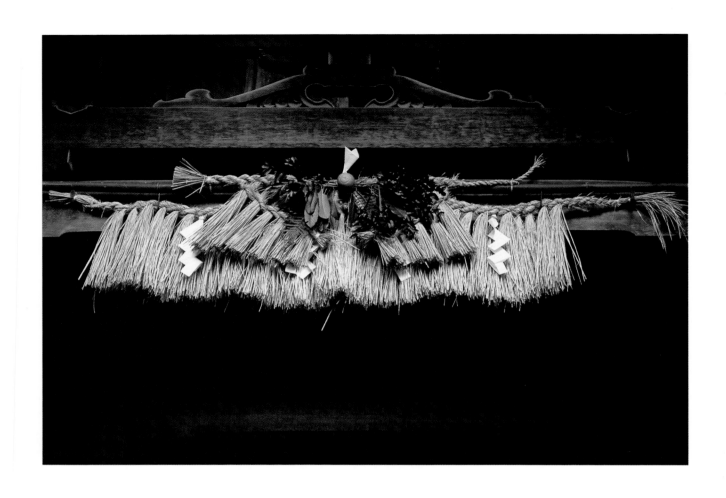

Opposite above The main shrine in Shikanoshima, a Kyushu fishing community, displays a double-layered *shimenawa*. The larger one will hang for the full year, but the smaller will be removed and burned at the end of the holiday season.

Opposite below Stone markers dedicated to various deities each receive an individual New Year decoration at Fushimi Inari Shrine in Kyoto.

Left In a modern update, the straw offering intended for the spirit of the well now hangs around the water spigot.

of Sanda's estate, a *shimenawa* decorated with a wooden plaque thought to have protective properties excited special interest, and at day's end, when the gates were about to close, hundreds would gather in the vain hope of obtaining the talisman.[9]

Although some local styles are disappearing, the regionalism that was obvious in *shimenawa* of the Edo period remains an important feature today, and each area produces at least three forms of *shimenawa*. The showiest, and generally the largest, are those designed for the entry gate or front door. Various good-luck symbols—sometimes so numerous that they conceal the straw form beneath— adorn the entryway *shimenawa*. A more sedate style, decorated only with folded strips of pristine white paper, is intended for the *kamidana* (main Shinto altar) and any of the smaller altars that may be found in the home. A third category includes smaller straw ornaments that are placed in various locations in and around the home as a symbol of thanks to the assorted *kami* who bless the running of the household. All are taken down at the end of the New Year's season except the altar decorations, which stay in place until renewed at the end of each year.[10]

Regionalism is further demonstrated in the type of good-luck symbols that decorate the doorway *shimenawa*. All express themes of good fortune, abundance, or longev-ity, and many take their meaning from the word plays that are common in Japanese. The three most prevalent decorations are fronds of a fern known as *urajiro*, leaves from the *yuzuriha* tree, and a bitter orange known as *daidai*. The fern is always turned to expose its whitish underside, demonstrating sincerity and purity of spirit; because its fronds spring in pairs from the stem, the plant also connotes marital harmony. The leaf of the *yuzuriha* does not fall until a new one is in place, auguring an unbroken transition from father to son. *Daidai*, whose homonym means generation to generation, carries a similar meaning. (Nobody seems to mind that an ordinary mandarin orange is nearly always substituted for the more expensive bitter orange.) Other adornments include: lobster, because its bent back signifies old age and the color red is a powerful demon repellent; folding paper fans, *suehiro*, because the spreadout form suggests expanding fortune and the word connotes many descendants; seaweeds, especially *konbu* and *hondawara*, which are word plays, the first alluding to the verb *yorokobu*, to rejoice, and the second hinting at the wealth and abundance implied by *tawara*, or rice bales; and dried persimmons, *kaki*, which also means "raking in," as of treasure.[11]

In addition to a decorative *shimenawa* for the entryway and (if the family follows traditional observance) one or

Above left Gold and silver foil-covered ties add refinement to an elegant Kyoto *shimenawa*.

Above right In the Ise area of Mie Prefecture, a "dragonfly" *shimenawa* is often paired with a branch of the sacred *sakaki* plant.

Opposite In the Kanazawa area, the entryway *shimenawa* is likened to a tortoise displaying its four legs and tail. The added decorations all relate to themes of health, long life, and prosperity.

more altar-style *shimenawa* for the household altars, many homeowners will purchase a set of small straw decorations known as *wakazari*, or straw circlets. For the most part these are modest loops of twisted straw, often decorated with a sprig of pine and a strip of cut and folded white paper, that are offered to the various *kami* who oversee the welfare of the household. These include the spirit of the well, who provides essential water for life and crops; the related deities of fire, the hearth, and the cooking pot, who supply heat and a means of cooking; the spirit of the privy, who protects the family from the pollution associated with this spot; and assorted other deities celebrated inside and outside the house. Modern Japanese have developed ingenious ways to honor these rustic-sounding spirits, and even in urban households it is not uncommon to find a small straw offering hanging on the kitchen faucet (for the "well" deity), near the water closet, next to the automatic rice cooker, or even on the gas or electric meter outside.[12]

Psychologically, these small offerings acknowledge the family's dependence on powers outside their control, and serve both to give thanks and petition for continued blessings. Since spiritual forces are thought to animate the material as well as the natural world, it is accepted practice to recognize one's indebtedness to utilitarian objects. This explains why such commonplace items as tools (from farm implements to computers) and vehicles (from bicycles and

Opposite *Shimenawa* designed for household use are often embellished with colorful decorations. Hung over the doorway or gate a few days before the end of the year, they generally stay in place through the first or second week of January. This bold example is from the Ueda region of Nagano Prefecture. (Private collection.)

Right A Shinto altar (*kamidana*) of the kind found in homes, shops, and occasionally even corporate offices. In preparation for the New Year, a new *shimenawa* and fresh green *sakaki* leaves are placed in the altar.

baby carriages to cars and buses) are often similarly adorned.

Until the late nineteenth century, when Japan was still primarily an agricultural nation, most New Year's *shimenawa* were made by individual farmers. Many proscriptions surrounded the process: the straw was to be grown in a special field, cut before the rice grains appeared, and dried in the shade to retain its green tinge; the rope was to be twisted on the last day of the year by the male head of the household, usually after undergoing some form of ritual purification, and no females or outsiders were to be present. There is no way to know how carefully such ritual prohibitions were followed, or whether farmers were tempted to wait for the precious rice to ripen before harvesting the straw.

Today most families purchase their decorations—at year-end markets, from supermarkets or flower stores, or from temporary stalls set up on nearby streets. Many farmers (or more accurately, farmers' wives, since the taboo against women seems to have been quietly forgotten) bring in a limited off-season profit by producing *shimenawa* to sell in nearby towns, while others have joined massive cooperatives that turn out numerous varieties, shipping them to cities that may be hundreds of miles away.

Changes in the postwar farming economy have resulted in a shortage of rice straw and that scarcity now threatens regional styles. As rice growing in Japan has been mechanized, productivity has increased, but machine-cut straw is unsuitable for *shimenawa*. To cope with the rice surplus, the government has ordered fields taken out of cultivation, making rice straw even scarcer. As farmers retire and sons and daughters take city jobs, no one is left to produce the local *shimenawa*, and the vacuum is filled by more dominant styles from nearby areas. Some of the demand is currently being met with imports from Korea, but vendors do their best to keep this fact secret so as not to offend customers who associate the *shimenawa* with hallowed native traditions.

Architecture poses an additional challenge to the continued use of *shimenawa*. The modern house, built of steel, glass, and concrete, offers no place to attach the decorations, and straw tassels that could once hang down in front of the traditional sliding door now get caught in the outward-opening Western-style doors. A new style of *shimenawa*—a sort of cross between a straw rope and a Christmas wreath—has recently come on the market, billing itself as the solution for the contemporary home. Such curiosities remain a novelty, however, and most people still prefer the traditional shapes they have known since childhood.

Four styles of undecorated *shimenawa*.

Opposite top A refined style for the household altar created by Honma Sakuzō of Yamagata Prefecture. (Private collection.)

Opposite bottom A Kyoto-style altar decoration by Nishikawa Katsuji. (Private collection.)

Above A traditional entryway *shimenawa* made by the late Suwa Otomatsu of Yamaguchi Prefecture in western Japan. (Private collection.)

Left A Tokyo-style *shimenawa* for the entryway. The handsome rice-straw base will be virtually concealed by a plethora of decorations. (Private collection.)

Above Vendors from the whole Kanto (greater Tokyo) region come to purchase *shimenawa* at the December wholesale market in downtown Tokyo. Each year Tokyo-style decorations are shipped farther and farther away, sometimes supplanting indigenous regional styles when local production declines.

Right *Tobi*, or workers involved in the construction trades, have controlled the distribution of New Year decorations in the capital since the Edo period. This circa 1920 photograph shows Tokyo's wholesale market just before the New Year.

Opposite November and December are busy months for the makers of New Year's *shimenawa*. Fujimoto Hideo of Yamaguchi Prefecture produces a special shape that incorporates the congratulatory character *kotobuki*.

A display at a year-end market in Kyoto, where unlike Tokyo, most vendors still produce their own *shimenawa*.

Opposite Outside a supermarket in Takayama (Gifu Prefecture), two women choose among brightly decorated local styles.

GUARDIANS OF THE GATE: *Kadomatsu*

The *kadomatsu*, a pine decoration that flanks the entrance gate, is so closely associated with the New Year that the days from January 1 to January 7 (or January 15, depending on local custom) are colloquially called "within the pines" (*matsu no uchi*).

In China the New Year custom of erecting pine boughs as a gate decoration dates to the sixth century, and still persists in outlying provinces.[13] While some scholars consider the *kadomatsu* an import from Tang-period China, the fact that the gate pine is not mentioned in Japanese texts until the eleventh century suggests that Chinese influence was more indirect. What did spread to Japan at an early date was symbolism concerning the evergreen. The Chinese viewed the pine as representing enduring life, a point of view that was reflected in Japan's first poetic anthology, the *Manyōshū* (compiled ca. 770). The Chinese association of the evergreen with the New Year is further seen in the Japanese folk practice of plucking rooted pine seedlings during the early days of year, an observance to ensure health and long life that had been incorporated into court ritual by the tenth century.[14]

Other forms of symbolism were unique to Japan. Like the sacred *sakaki* tree, the pine was thought of as a vehicle for the passage of divine spirits into and out of this world. In this context, it shared the heritage of the cult sticks or ritual poles used as a kind of spirit lightning rod

by the peoples of Northeast Asia. At the New Year, the gate pine's most important role was to summon the year-god into the household, bringing his numerous blessings, and to offer its branches as an abode during his stay. In some parts of Japan, straw decorations suggesting containers are still attached to the kadomatsu to hold real or symbolic food offerings for the spirit residing there.

Like the straw shimenawa, the kadomatsu originated in popular practice and later spread to the upper classes. In the twelfth-century picture scroll that offers the earliest extant illustration of the New Year kadomatsu (the same scroll that first illustrates the shimenawa), pine trees are erected only in front of commoners' homes.[15] By the fourteenth century the custom was so widespread that writer Yoshida Kenkō singled out the festive scene created by "the main thoroughfares, decorated their full length with pine boughs."[16] Though the kadomatsu was taken up by the warrior classes, it was never adopted by the highest nobility, and even today pine decorations will not be found at the gates to the Imperial Palace.

Over the years, kadomatsu have undergone numerous changes. Early paintings show what appear to be whole pine trees, their bases secured in the ground at either side of a dwelling's entryway. In about the fourteenth century bamboo, a metaphor for life extending "ten thousand years," was added to the arrangement. In illustrations of the sixteenth century onward, kindling—considered a

talisman against ill fortune—is often seen buttressing the foot of the pine and bamboo. Split wood is still a feature of kadomatsu in certain parts of the country, but in Edo (Tokyo) the practice of wrapping the kindling with straw rope led to the straw-covered base common in eastern Japan today.[17]

The use of kadomatsu was neither universal nor standardized before the modern era. Certain areas, including Osaka and Toyama, had no tradition of pine decorations. In other regions branches of sakaki or other plants were displayed, or a single pine was erected within the house rather than the customary pair at the entrance. In the capital of Edo some curious variations existed. Stalks of giant green bamboo stood on either side of the gate to the Lord of Hirosaki's residence, while Lord Satake of Akita, shunning kadomatsu entirely, had vassals in formal dress line the entryway in a display renowned as "Satake's human gate pines." In the pleasure quarters of Yoshiwara, the gate pines were turned to face inward, as a kind of charm to entice customers to extend their stay.[18]

Regional variations still abound in the countryside, but in most urban areas a single style has become dominant. The typical kadomatsu now consists of three (or occasionally five) large stalks of green bamboo, their tops cut at a slant, thrust in a base of bushy pine branches. This particular style, which derived from the gate pines that once stood at the entrances to Edo castle, gained national

recognition at the end of the nineteenth century when it was celebrated in a children's song that was incorporated in the country's newly established school curriculum. Displayed at schools and government offices, the formal *kadomatsu* quickly became the prevailing style throughout the country.[19]

According to the traditional calendar, which sets aside a particular day for nearly every ritual activity, the pines for *kadomatsu* are to be cut in the hills on the thirteenth day of the last month and set aside until the gate decorations are erected on an auspicious day shortly before the New Year. Because cutting the branches for *kadomatsu* is considered a sacred activity, entry into otherwise private land is supposedly condoned. In contrast to rural practice, city dwellers have long had to rely on vendors for their New Year's supply of pine branches. By the latter part of the Edo period, labor bosses in the construction trades (known as *tobi*, or "hawks," for their ability to scale tall heights) came to have a virtual monopoly on the supply of New Year's decorations in the capital, and even today the erection of *kadomatsu* in many Tokyo districts remains in the hands of the descendants of these professionals.[20]

Changes in postwar circumstances and philosophy have resulted in significant alterations in the use of *kadomatsu*. Current building materials are unfriendly to the decora-

Opposite The pine is an ancient symbol of longevity and seasonal regeneration. Split logs or kindling, once considered a talisman against evil, still form the base of this *kadomatsu* from the old town of Tsumago in Nagano Prefecture.

Above left Most contemporary *kadomatsu* incorporate three stalks of bamboo cut at a slant; only the wrapping material for the base hints at regional differences. Modern *kadomatsu* are modeled after the pine arrangements that once stood in front of Edo castle. This formal variation is from the city of Okayama.

Above right A straw-wrapped base is typical of *kadomatsu* of the Tokyo region, but the style has spread to other parts of the country as well. In northern Japan Onodera Masaji, a farmer and craftsman, fashions impressive Tokyo-style arrangements for local hospitals and institutions.

Left Workers in Tokyo fashion a huge arrangement of bamboo and pine at either side of the popular downtown temple known as Asakusa Kannon. These *kadomatsu*, or gate pines, are thought to summon the year-god and provide him a place of residence during his New Year sojourn.

Right Many homes in Kyoto display simple *kadomatsu* of uprooted pine seedlings. The decorations recall the Heian-period ritual of plucking pine seedlings in the first days of spring to help ensure longevity.

Opposite An offering dedicated to the mountain god is one of a set of eight *gohei*, or sacred cut-paper pendants, made for parishioners by Kiyohara Masao, priest of Onga Hachiman Shrine in Miyagi Prefecture. One is used to purify the house on New Year's Eve, the others are placed on the altar or offered at locations where the various deities reside. (Honolulu Academy of Arts, gift of Kiyohara Masao, 1993.)

tions, providing few places to secure them, and dirt entryways into which large pine boughs could be inserted have mostly been paved over. Showy *kadomatsu*, especially in the countryside, have been slowly vanishing from individual residences, replaced by more modest arrangements. Under the influence of the "New Life Movement," a reform program with environmental overtones that began in the 1950s, a few communities have even abandoned *kadomatsu* entirely in favor of printed paper images pasted on each side of the doorway. By contrast, arrangements in urban areas have tended to become more elaborate, and today the most impressive *kadomatsu* tend to be found in front of commercial buildings, from banks and hotels to department stores and game parlors. While they may no longer be viewed as vessels of divine power, these public displays are still handsome symbols of the New Year, as well as vivid reminders of the shared cultural traditions the season celebrates.

ALTAR DECORATIONS OF PAPER AND BAMBOO

The sacred origins of the familiar and conspicuous entryway decorations of pine and straw may have become obscured, but there is no doubt about the spiritual symbolism of another group of ornaments, the emblems associated with household worship, and in particular with the household

In the Kurihara area of Miyagi Prefecture, paper figures representing the gods of the eight directions are distributed to shrine members by Kiyohara Masao. The figures hang in the kitchen near the small altar dedicated to the hearth spirit. (Honolulu Academy of Arts, gift of Kiyohara Masao, 1993.)

altar or *kamidana*. Produced in limited quantities in scattered communities throughout the country, these special altar decorations retain a strong regional flavor.

Kirigami: Decorations of Cut Paper

Paper has been closely linked with the sacred since papermaking was first introduced to Japan sometime between the fifth and seventh centuries. Fibers of the hemp and paper mulberry plants were important ritual offerings long before they were used as raw materials for papermaking, and so paper naturally inherited a similar function. Shinto ceremonies, codified in the tenth century, include scattering cut paper as a means of purifying a ritual site, and records show that early travelers carried a mix of cut paper, rice, and *sakaki* leaves that could help to placate unfriendly spirits encountered far from home. Paper charms printed with mystical words or symbols were also coveted for the magical protection they provided against evil forces.[21]

Certain paper items are a familiar element of New Year custom and ritual. These include *shide*, the cut and folded white paper streamers that hang down from the *shimenawa*, and *ofuda*, paper placards bearing the name or image of a deity along with the name of the issuing shrine or temple. Conscientious worshipers generally purchase new placards at the New Year, placing them on the home

The *gohei* cut by Gunji Mitsuho, priest of Komine Shrine in Miyagi Prefecture, bear the motifs of the ox and the rat, two of the twelve zodiac-year animals. (Honolulu Academy of Arts, gift of Gunji Mitsuho, 1993.)

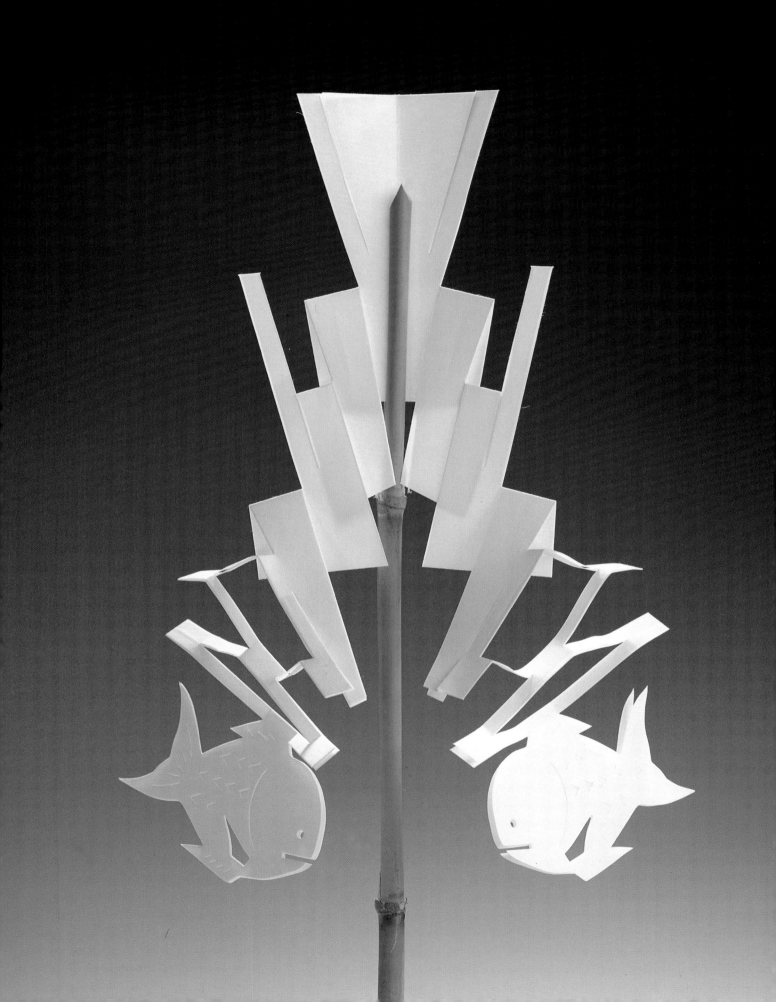

altar or attaching them to doorposts, lintels, or even outbuildings to assure the deities' protective benevolence during the coming year. Some shrines still perform an ancient year-end purification rite in which simple figures cut from white paper are rubbed over the body and then burnt or washed away in a stream, symbolically cleansing the worshiper of past defilement and preparing him to receive the blessings of the New Year.[22] Beyond these customary paper articles, fairly uniform in shape and function throughout the country, much more elaborate paper decorations that preserve a great deal of regional variation are found in certain parts of Japan. Known under the general name of *kirigami*, or cut paper, these are mainly altar decorations that range from quaint folk cuttings to intricate, lacy hangings many feet in length. The designs they incorporate are delightfully lighthearted: the smiling visages of the deities of good fortune, Ebisu and Daikoku; symbols of longevity such as the crane and tortoise; trays piled high with bounty from field and sea; and even representations of coins and money bags. Taken together, the motifs reflect a boundless optimism concerning the new year, as well as an unshakable faith in the willingness of the deities to busy themselves with the everyday concerns of humankind.

The history of the paper decorations and how they

Opposite Fish are a symbol of the lucky god Ebisu, who guarantees a good catch to fisherman and prosperity to merchants. This cut-paper pendant, from Mishima Grand Shrine in Shizuoka Prefecture, is renewed annually at the New Year. (Private collection.)

Above In Miyagi Prefecture, a small shrine to the god of livestock receives a special paper decoration. New Year paper cuttings are found in scattered regions throughout Japan, but the tradition is richest in the north.

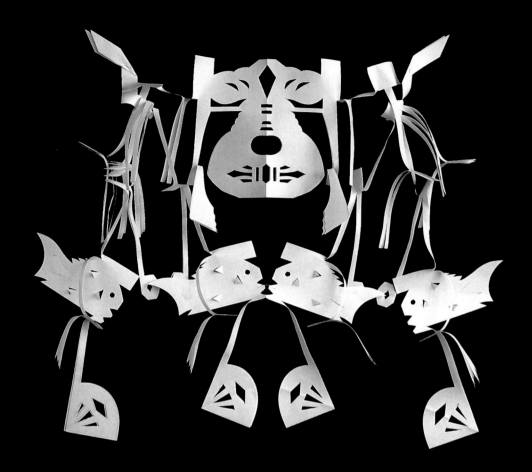

Opposite top A raised wooden stand holds a sacred treasure bag and seeds of the "five grains" of agricultural prosperity. Cut by Kudō Sukeyoshi, priest of Kaminoyama Shrine in northern Japan, it belongs to a set of four designed to hang in front of the New Year altar. (Honolulu Academy of Arts, gift of Kudō Sukeyoshi, 1993.)

Opposite bottom The god of the New Year, symbolized by a cut-paper *gohei*, arrives on the back of a sacred horse. Priest Abe Takeshi of Hakusan Shrine in Miyagi Prefecture prepares this design to hang in front of various household altars. (Honolulu Academy of Arts, gift of Abe Takeshi, 1993.)

Above Lacy paper cuttings may be hung either in front of or over the New Year altar. In this example by Abe Takeshi of Hakusan Shrine, motifs of good fortune and prosperity abound. (Honolulu Academy of Arts, gift of Abe Takeshi, 1993.)

came to be associated with the New Year celebration is not well documented. Paper remained a luxury good in limited supply until the late seventeenth century, so the decorations could not have come into popular use before then. Geographical distribution remains a puzzle as well: although various styles of *kirigami* are found in scattered locations on all of Japan's main islands, most originate in the area from Kyoto eastward, with by far the greatest concentration in the Tohoku region of northern Japan.[23] In some areas *kirigami* are sold commercially in year-end markets, but most of the decorations, especially in Tohoku, continue to be cut and distributed by Shinto priests.

The prevalence of *kirigami* in the cold north may be related to climate: here, at least until the technological advances of the Meiji period, rice did not flourish, and paper was welcomed as an alternative to scarce rice straw for the New Year decorations. The *yamabushi*, itinerant monks practicing a syncretic mix of esoteric Buddhism and mountain worship who served as healers and exorcists in many Tohoku communities, used paper cutouts in their sacred dance and may have spread the art form to the populace at large. In 1873 the new Meiji government—seeking to bolster the emperor's claim to divinity and promote the Shinto faith on which it was based—pro-

scribed the *yamabushi* sect as part of a campaign to purge Buddhist elements from Shinto. Deprived of their traditional livelihood, many of the monks became Shinto priests, and today in northern Japan their descendants carry on the tradition of dispersing cut-paper decorations to parishioners at the New Year.[24]

There are three basic styles of New Year's *kirigami*. First (and most ancient) are *gohei*, geometrical "lightning-shaped" pendants produced by cutting and folding strips of paper and inserting them in a split bamboo wand. *Gohei* have a dual aspect—they are both an offering and an object of worship that embodies the spirit of a particular deity. *Gohei* representing the year-god are placed on the New Year altar, while those honoring other deities may be found in the kitchen, near the well, and on various outbuildings where the assorted *kami* are thought to reside. Though they are generally left in place the whole year, *gohei* are always renewed in late December, and for this reason they are intimately tied to the New Year season.[25]

Rectangular paper cutouts, usually pictorial representations of benevolent deities or good-luck symbols designed to hang from the front of the wooden shelf that constitutes the household altar are another form of New Year *kirigami*. A third style combines pictorial and geomet-

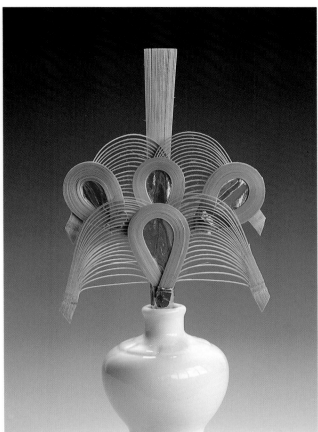

ric techniques in elaborate lacy nets from which images of fish, rice bales, and other motifs of plenty are suspended. Hung above the New Year's altar as a replacement for the rice-straw *shimenawa*, these elaborate streamers can stretch as much as eight feet in length. It is easy to see how such festive decorations could help dispel the gloom of the dark northern winter and console the household with thoughts of the coming spring.

As the year draws to a close, the priests of Tohoku—along with their Shinto and Buddhist counterparts in other areas where *kirigami* is preserved as a New Year tradition—find themselves busily engaged in paper cutting. Each priest preserves a different style, but designs may change as the art is passed from generation to generation. Fewer varieties are made today, both because of decreasing demand (a farmer who turns to a city job, for instance, may no longer feel obligated to honor the gods of the field or of livestock) and because the burden of the job has caused a number of priests either to forsake the practice or to use metal dies that stamp out identical forms in a fraction of the time it takes to cut them by hand. In the communities where the craft is preserved, however, the cheery white decorations are considered an integral part of the holiday and are not likely to be lightly abandoned.

Opposite A householder in Iwate Prefecture prepares to place a New Year's paper cutting above the household altar. The neighborhood priest, who once cut this design of coins and rice bales by hand, now uses a metal die to speed his work.

Above left *Miki no kuchi*, altar decorations inserted in the containers that hold ceremonial offerings of sake, are produced from wood shavings in Aomori. The delicate shape suggests the flickering flame of a candle. (Honolulu Academy of Arts, purchase, 1992.)

Above right An exquisite altar decoration of split bamboo from Toyama. (Honolulu Academy of Arts, gift of Endō Chūkō, 1992.)

Opposite An elegant paper *miki no kuchi* from Sakata in Yamagata Prefecture. (Private collection.)

The sacred aspect of a New Year offering of pounded rice cakes on display in a Kyoto restaurant is emphasized by the presence of a pair of *miki no kuchi* in porcelain sake containers.

Miki no kuchi: Bamboo Filaments

Among the decorations renewed at the end of the year are the delicate altar offerings known as miki no kuchi, literally "mouth of the sacred wine," which are ornaments inserted into the narrow opening of containers that hold ceremonial offerings of sake. Sake offerings are placed in pairs on the household altar, in front of the tokonoma (living room alcove), or in any number of other locations where the spirits are to be welcomed. As a derivative of rice, sake is itself a sacred offering much loved by the kami. Intoxication at the time of festivals or religious rituals is not only tolerated in Japan but is often encouraged, for it is said that when men and the gods drink together they become bonded in celebration. Since the god of the New Year also bears responsibility for the rice crop, no offering could be more appropriate for the season.

Miki no kuchi can be made from various materials—paper, shaved or sculpted wood, or even metal—but those of bamboo are most plentiful and display the greatest variety. Crafted from bamboo stalks that are harvested in November, then split and shaped into elaborate designs in time for the year-end markets, the graceful ornaments are treasured for their touch of springlike green.

Ethnographers surmise that miki no kuchi share the heritage of gohei (paper streamers) and pine: both are implements to invoke the gods. The few historical records that exist suggest that the prototype may have been an ornament of shaved wood created in the Nara region some three hundred years ago. In a revealing print of 1798, a peddler of paper miki no kuchi is seen chatting with a vendor of New Year's pine decorations, an indication that the ornament had become associated with the holiday by the end of the eighteenth century.[26]

According to Okamura Kichiemon, a scholar whose collection of miki no kuchi is one of Japan's finest, these objects were most popular from the last half of the nineteenth through the second decade of the twentieth century, when over three hundred varieties have been documented. Since the 1930s usage has declined, precipitously in the postwar years. The declining use of kamidana in the home and the rising cost of these intricate and labor-intensive decorations are factors that have affected production. With the exception of isolated craftsmen, the manufacture of miki no kuchi has virtually disappeared from western Japan; in the region from Kyoto eastward production is limited to certain scattered communities.[27]

What happens to all the decorations of the New Year after they have served their purpose? Around January 7, or later depending on local custom, the pine branches and rice-straw ropes are taken down from the gates and door-

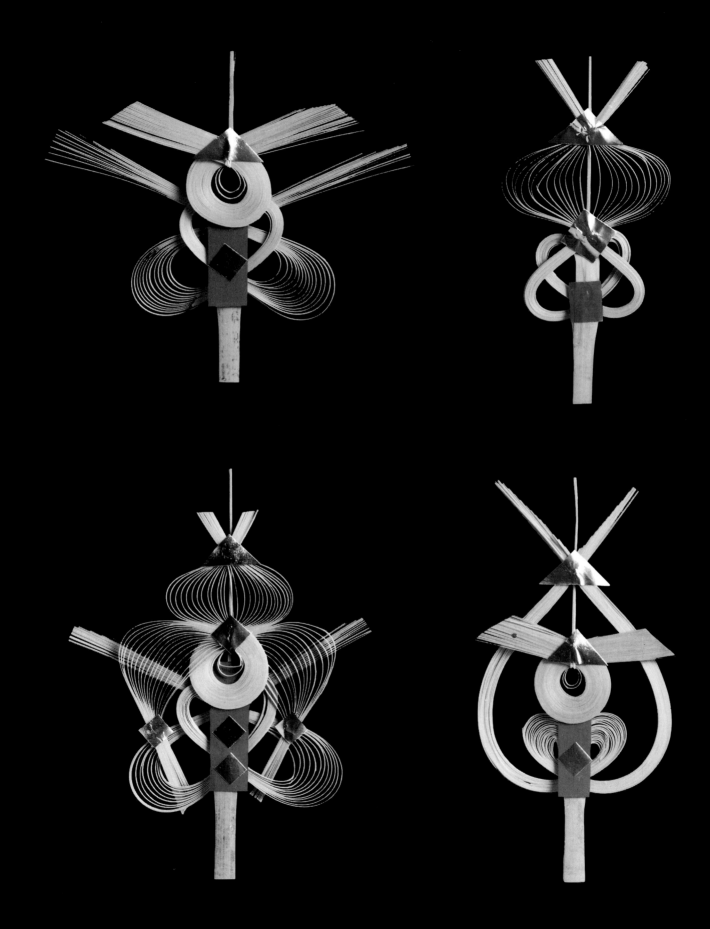

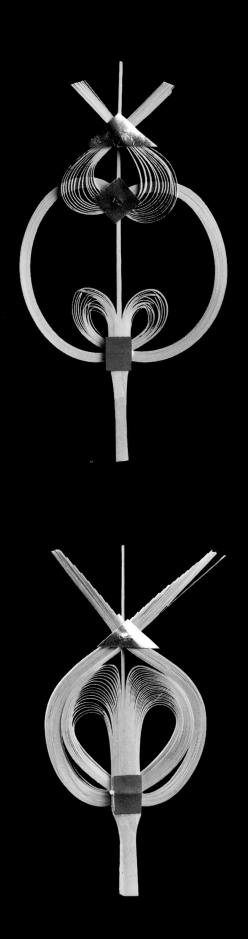

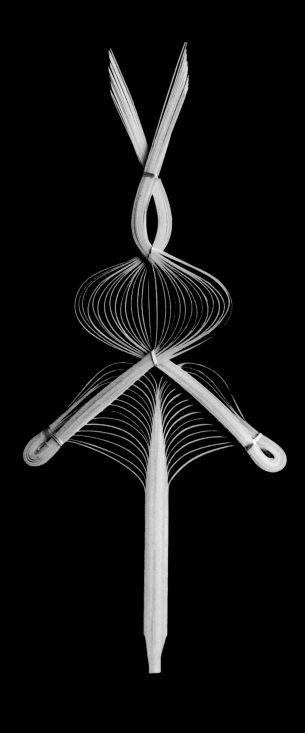

Bamboo *miki no kuchi* from various locations.

Opposite   Four examples from Ōme, Tokyo.

Top left   Hinode, Tokyo.

Left   Fussa, Tokyo.

Above   Sendai, Miyagi Prefecture. (Private collection.)

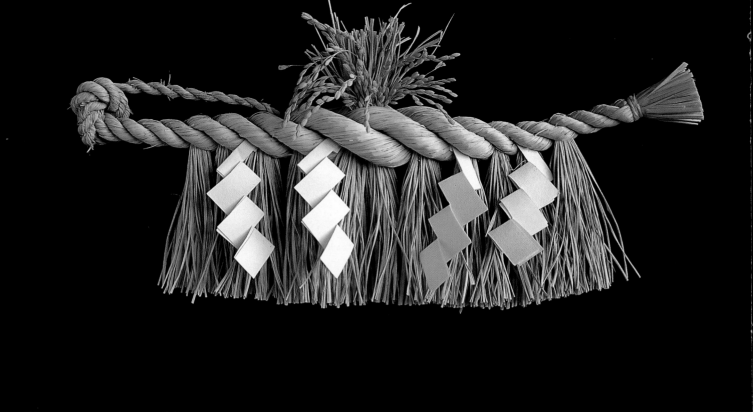

Altar-style *shimenawa* from Niigata Prefecture. (Private collection.)

A *shimenawa*-style girdle of twisted white fabric is worn by high-ranking sumo wrestlers during formal appearances, recalling the fact that the ancient sport originated as an entertainment for the gods. Grand champions are known as *yokozuna* (lit. "horizontal rope") after this special ceremonial belt.

ways.[28] The Japanese rarely talk of "throwing away" or "discarding" them. Instead they use the word *osameru*, to lay to rest, implying that something is restored to its appropriate place. In popular thought, the New Year's decorations, along with the assorted talismans and amulets accumulated during the previous year, represent a reservoir of spiritual power borrowed from the *kami*. They bring good luck and protect the household by absorbing misfortune, but when their power is spent they are returned to their source.

Flames generally accomplish this, whether through a community bonfire or through a householder's match. In urban areas, where open burning is strictly regulated, many people carry everything to a neighborhood shrine. Here, either at a public ceremony that is likely to coincide with the January 15 celebration of the Little New Year or quietly at the shrine's convenience, these objects of ephemeral beauty are put to the flame. As the smoke rises, it carries away any last cares and grievances, thus bringing the season to a purified close.[29]

1. Buddhism in Japan is known as the religion of funerals, and it is this connection with death (considered a defilement in Shinto thought) that explains why Buddhist monks were once considered unwelcome guests during the festivities of the New Year. The observation was recorded in the early seventeenth century by João Rodrigues, S.J., cited in Michael Cooper, *They Came to Japan: An Anthology of European Reports on Japan, 1543–1640* (Berkeley and Los Angeles: University of California Press, 1965), 357.

2. Wakamori, *Nenchū gyōji*, 11.

3. Shibusawa Keizō, ed. *Emakimono ni yoru Nihon jōmin seikatsu ebiki* (Index to daily life as seen in picture scrolls) (Tokyo: Heibonsha, 1984), 2:37, 53, 60–62, 226–27, 3:68, 5:86. Boundary ropes, customarily renewed around the time of the celebration known as the Little New Year, are still found in Nara, Hyogo, and Chiba Prefectures.

4. Donald Philippi, ed. and trans., *Kojiki* (Princeton, NJ, and Tokyo: Princeton University Press and Tokyo University Press, 1969), 81–86.

5. Torigoe Kenzaburō, *Unnan kara no michi: Nihon no ruutsu o saguru* (The road from Yunnan: searching for Japan's roots) (Tokyo: Kōdansha, 1983), 74–78; Imamura Tomo, "Chōsen no kenjō to Nihon no shimenawa ni tsuite" (On relations between *inchul* in Korea and *shimenawa* in Japan), Part 1, *Minzokugaku* 3 (1931): 21–26; Choe, *Annual Customs of Korea*, 43, 47, 49, 81.

6. Miyazaki, *Wara*, 2:268–70; Moriya Mitsuo, ed. and trans., *Keiso saijiki* (Annual events of the state of Chu), a translation of *Jing chu sui shi ji* by Zong Lin (Tokyo: Tōyō Bunko, 1982), 10–11.

7. Helen Craig McCullough, ed. & trans., *Kokin Wakashū: The First Imperial Anthology of Japanese Poetry, with Tosa Nikki and Shinsen Waka* (Stanford, CA: Stanford University Press, 1985), 268.

8. Yuzuriha, Lat. *Daphniphyllum macropodum*. See Kadokawa Shoten, ed., *Nenchū gyōji emaki*, 3.

9. The Saga fief was in northern Kyushu; the Nambu clan governed lands in Tohoku (northern Japan). Sanda is near present-day Osaka, but the lord's ancestors came from the Ise area, where the tradition of decorating *shimenawa* with wooden amulets still continues. Ishikawa, *Edo bungaku zokushin jiten*, 81–82; Nishitsunoi, *Nenchū gyōji jiten*, 200–203.

10. In the Ise area and certain parts of Chiba Prefecture entryway *shimenawa* are left up for a full year.

11. Urajiro (lit. "underside white"), Lat. *Gleichenia japonica*; *daidai* (bigarade), Lat. *Citrus aurantium*. Yuzuriha and urajiro were in use since the Heian period (794–1185), whereas *daidai* and most other decorations date from the Edo period. Nihon fūzokushi gakkai, ed., *Nihon fūzokushi jiten* (Dictionary of the history of Japanese customs) (Tokyo: Kōbundō, 1979), 280–281.

12. In the 1890s, when piped water was first becoming widely available in Tokyo, some observers grumbled that the straw decoration meant to honor the well god looked out of place on a "modern" appliance like a water spigot, but few today seem concerned with the apparent incongruity. Tsuchida Mitsufumi, *Meiji Tokyo saijiki* (Glossary of seasonal references concerning Tokyo in the Meiji period) (Tokyo: Seiabō, 1968), 128.

13. Moriya, *Keiso saijiki*, 10–11.

14. The plucking of pine seedlings occurred on the first Day of the Rat, and also involved the collection of herbs thought to ward off illness. By the eleventh century the observance had shifted to the seventh of the first month, the date that even today is set aside for eating the health-giving "seven herbs" (*nanakusa*). William H. and Helen Craig McCullough, eds. and trans., *A Tale of Flowering Fortunes: Annals of Japanese Aristocratic Life in the Heian Period* (Stanford, CA: Stanford University Press, 1980), 383; and Morris, *The World of the Shining Prince*, 158 n. 1.

15. Kadokawa Shoten, ed., *Nenchū gyōji emaki*, 3.

16. Donald Keene, ed. & trans., *Essays in Idleness: The Tsurezuregusa of Kenkō* (New York and London: Columbia University Press, 1967), 21.

17. Kadokawa Shoten, ed., *Nenchū gyōji emaki*, 3; Hayashi Tatsusaburō, *Kyō no shiki* (The four seasons of Kyoto) (Tokyo: Iwanami Shoten, 1985), 10–11; Mitani Kazuma, ed., *Ukiyoe: Edo no ichinen* (A year in the life of Edo through ukiyoe prints) (Tokyo: Ōta Memorial Museum of Art, 1988). The addition of plum to form the auspicious triad known as *shōchikubai* occurred only in the Meiji period (1868–1912).

18. Ishikawa, *Edo bungaku zokushin jiten*, 81; Kadokawa Shoten, ed., *Zusetsu haiku daisaijiki*, 5:92; Nishitsunoi, *Nenchū gyōji jiten*, 202.

19. Hashiura Yasuo, *Matsuri to gyōji* (Festivals and ceremonies) (Tokyo: Mainichi Shinbunsha, 1949), 19–20.

20. *Kadomatsu* vendors appear in handscrolls as early as the thirteenth century. See Shibusawa, *Emakimono ni yoru Nihon jōmin seikatsu ebiki*, 3:59. For the role of the *tobi*, see Tsuchida, *Meiji Tokyo saijiki*, 128, and Bestor, *Neighborhood Tokyo*, 307.

21. Felicia Gressitt Bock, ed. and trans., *Engi-shiki: Procedures of the Engi Era* (Tokyo: Sophia University, 1970), 1: 66; William George Aston, *Shinto: The Way of the Gods* (London and New York: Longmans, Green, 1905), 216.

22. The purification ceremony is an outgrowth of a ritual adopted from China; in the Heian period it was performed at court on the last day of the sixth and twelfth months as a means of ridding the entire nation of defilement. Although the December rite continues to be performed at many shrines, it lost some of its popularity after the twelfth or thirteenth century, making the mid-summer purification the better-known ceremony. Bock, ed. and trans., *Engi-shiki*, 1:3.

23. Other areas known for New Year's *kirigami* include Niigata, the Noto Peninsula, certain towns in Yamanashi Prefecture, the Izumo area of Shimane Prefecture, and Mt. Kōya (a center of Shingon Buddhism in Wakayama Prefecture).

24. Kumagai Seiji, "Inori no denshō kirigami" (Traditional Japanese paper cutting), *Ginka* 32 (Winter 1977): 1–3; Kamekura, "Nihon no kirigami: shōgatsu kazari," 3–6.

25. For a discussion of the history and use of *gohei* see Contemporary Religions in Japan, ed., "Shinto Symbols (Part II)," 93–96. Scenes from picture scrolls showing *gohei* offerings made by twelfth-century travelers can be found in Shibusawa, *Emakimono ni yoru Nihon jōmin seikatsu ebiki*, 1:3, 111.

26. Fuchū City Kyōdo no Mori, ed., *Miki no kuchi: Okamura korekushon o chūshin ni*, 13.

27. Ibid., 8–9. For further information see also Okamura, "Miki no kuchi zuisō," and Saitama Prefectural Museum, ed., *Katadorareta inori*.

28. It was once standard practice to leave the pine and straw decorations in place at least until the fifteenth of the first month. In Edo (Tokyo), however, the fire danger posed by the drying decorations caused the government as early as the mid-seventeenth century to order that the date for removal be pushed to the 7th. Kitagawa Morisada, *Morisada Mankō* (A miscellany by Morisada), ed. Asakura Haruhiko and Kashikawa Shūichi (1867; reprint, Tokyo: Tōkyōdo Shuppan, 1992), 4:89–90. In the twentieth century pressure to shorten the New Year season increased, and communities that leave the ornaments in place through the second week of January are now in the minority. Kadokawa Shoten, ed., *Zusetsu haiku daisaijiki*, 5:154–55.

29. Not every item receives such decorous treatment. Large shrines that collect mountains of ornaments may choose one portion for ceremonial burning, then have the rest disposed of. From the worshipper's point of view, however, the action of bringing the decorations to the shrine fulfills the condition of returning them to the gods, so the details of ultimate disposal may not be of particular concern.

III

Koshōgatsu
The Farmers' Little New Year

Enbutsu Sumiko

THE CALENDAR imported from China in A.D. 604 measured time by the phases of the moon, with New Year's Day—and the first of each month thereafter—coinciding with the new moon. For centuries after the Chinese system was adopted at court, however, most Japanese continued the native practice of celebrating the start of the year at the full moon two weeks later.[1] Not until the mid-Edo period (ca. 1700), when the New Year practices of the court and government began to spread to all classes, was it necessary to distinguish between the two holidays. In contrast to the official or Greater New Year (*ōshōgatsu*), the mid-month celebration came to be known as Full Moon New Year or Little New Year (*koshōgatsu*). While the former is a rather formal observance deriving from practices of the imperial court and elite warriors who took pride in following Chinese customs, the Little New Year is a rustic agricultural festival thought to retain traces of the ancient practices of indigenous Japanese.[2]

To the early Japanese, the lunar cycle offered a convenient counter for marking time and the full moon was a welcome source of light. To the farmer, the first full moon of the year also marked the turning point from winter to spring, so it possessed particular ritual significance. During this auspicious time, when the farmer was least occupied

A winding road leads into the mountains of Chichibu, a district rich in local traditions. Observances of the mid-January holiday known as the Little New Year have vanished from most urban areas, but remain an important element in isolated rural communities.

Opposite The theme of gods in strange disguises entering the community at the Little New Year is found in various communities throughout Japan. In the Namahage rite of the Oga Peninsula in Akita Prefecture, young men dressed in straw coats and fierce masks visit each village household. By extending the gods hospitality, the householder invites good fortune and ensures a good harvest.

Left Farmers' concerns with productivity are central to the Little New Year celebration. Branches decorated with rice-flour dumplings resemble trees in full bloom and suggest a fruitful harvest. In regions like Chichibu where the silk industry once thrived, the dumplings are likened to silk cocoons.

Right Rolling two dumplings at once is a ritual practice that suggests fertility. Women were once excluded from this sacred task, but because of a shortage of hands they have now largely replaced men.

Opposite top Families that celebrate the Little New Year take down the pine and straw decorations on January 14 and replace them with rice dumpling offerings and ornaments of carved wood. In the Isoda household (Higashi Chichibu, Saitama Prefecture), the movable altar is repositioned each New Year to greet the year-god's arrival from the appropriate "lucky direction."

Opposite bottom In the Uchida household, dumplings on plum branches are offered to the benevolent gods Ebisu and Daikoku, as well as to other spirits that protect the family.

with chores, it became customary to celebrate the renewal of the agricultural year and pray for a bountiful harvest in the year to come. Japan's farming population clung to the custom of welcoming spring when the moon was full, long after the Chinese custom of celebrating the first day of the first month had been adopted at court.

In both Chinese and Japanese thought, the start of the year also marked the beginning of spring and was a time of great ritual importance. Since the official New Year generally fell at the second new moon after the winter solstice— a date whose equivalent in the western solar calendar ranged from late January to mid-February—the weather was naturally still cold.[3] Some scholars feel that the Japanese farmer originally observed the New Year at a full moon one or two months later when the burgeoning signs of spring were more perceptible. According to this theory, as the calendar spread to the masses an earlier date was gradually accepted as the start of the year, but farmers continued to focus their celebration in the middle of the month because of the full moon's symbolic importance.[4]

When the new Meiji government abandoned the lunar cycle as a way of measuring time and adopted the solar or Gregorian calendar of the West in the late nineteenth century, it caused considerable confusion in the dating of traditional holidays. The Greater New Year was

A youngster stands near the living room alcove filled with wooden offerings carved by her grandfather. The wooden offerings will be removed on January 16 and burned shortly thereafter; the dumplings will be boiled or roasted.

Opposite left A Little New Year display in Saitama Prefecture features auspicious scrolls, "silk cocoons" (rice-flour dumplings) on branches, a fortune-beckoning cat, and a bright red *daruma*.

Opposite right In the village of Shiiba in Miyazaki Prefecture an impressive display known as "celebrating the crops" combines millet heads with carved wooden branches, rice cake "flowers," and a straw pouch holding rice. Little New Year decorations vary by region, but all are designed to celebrate the coming of spring and express the farmer's prayer for a bountiful harvest.

pushed back approximately one month to January 1, and *koshōgatsu*, losing its link to the full moon, came to fall two weeks later on January 15. Despite the incongruity of welcoming spring even before the coldest days of the year had arrived, communities slowly accepted the change, and today virtually all the observances of the Little New Year occur on or around January 15.

Once observed throughout the country, *koshōgatsu* has succumbed to industrialization and is now generally celebrated in attenuated form as an adjunct to the January 1 holiday. Aspects of the holiday have been absorbed into numerous festivals, religious rites, and folk observances that occur from January well into April. The core of the Little New Year observance, however, is January 14–16, and all signs of the celebration generally vanish by January 20. Still largely untouched by commercialization, the quiet rituals of this period highlight the agrarian traditions that played a central role in shaping Japanese culture.

Koshōgatsu customs differ throughout the country, but most fall into two basic categories. First are the various productivity rites designed to entice energy from the earth and assure a bountiful year. Second are the divination rituals, aimed at discerning the pleasure of the *kami* and predicting the outcome of the harvest. These observances are often accompanied by ceremonies relating to gods of

good fortune who visit in disguise, and by fire rites that symbolically inoculate the community against evil forces and ritually divide the year.

RITES OF AGRICULTURAL RENEWAL

The New Year festival reveals a concept of time that springs from Japan's agrarian past, namely, that time, like the seasons, is cyclical, something that ends and must be regenerated. Farmers used ritual and repetition as magical tools to revitalize the year, in the belief that ritually enacting an event could induce it to occur.

Imitative magic colors many of the Little New Year rituals. In Aomori, for instance, pea pods are scattered in the yard at night to represent sowing; in Iwate small sprigs of pine are "planted" in the snow to pantomime the transplanting of rice seedlings in May; and in Nagano chants are sung by children to "chase away the birds" that prey on the rice crop in late summer.[5] Even under the old calendar, when *koshōgatsu* took place much closer to the solar spring, these ceremonies were performed far in advance of the events they mimic. Enacted under the light of the year's first full moon, however, they promised to revitalize the seasons, ensure the smooth progression of agricultural operations, and keep at bay those forces that could threaten the harvest.

Nowadays the rites of ceremonial reenactment are often observed later in spring rather than at the Little New Year, but there is a related ritual activity that has remained closely tied to the mid-January holiday. *Monotsukuri*, or "making things," involves the creation of decorations that emulate crops in full flower or fruit. These images of bounty are placed at various locations around the house and grounds as offerings that challenge the various crops to match them in productivity.

The most familiar *koshōgatsu* decorations are branches laden with rice dumplings. Like all the Little New Year offerings, they are made in large quantities because abundance signals the richness of life for which farmers pray. Depending on the region, the raw material will be either *mochi* (glutinous rice that is steamed and then pounded) or rice flour that is rolled into balls and then boiled. In many areas the bedecked branches are referred to as rice-cake "flowers" (*mochibana*), but in regions where silk sericulture is practiced they are more commonly called *mayudama*, "silk cocoons."

In Chichibu, a rural region northwest of Tokyo, a kind of fertility magic is observed when preparing the dumplings, with two balls shaped at once to represent male and female forces. Women were once considered ritually impure and thus ineligible for this task, but today such attitudes have weakened and pragmatism prevails, so women generally have replaced men at such tasks. Decorated branches are offered to a variety of household deities, but the most splendid display—a small tree including its rooted base—is reserved for the *tokonoma* alcove in the drawing room. Representing prosperity firmly rooted in the house, this lucky tree once filled the whole space before the alcove. Such extravagance is rare today, in part because the dumplings would likely go to waste. In former days of hardship the dumplings were treasured as a crunchy snack or hoarded as an emergency ration, but in the present age of affluence the plain food seems to have lost much of its appeal.

At the end of the *koshōgatsu* celebration, most commonly on January 16th but generally no later than the 20th, the decorated branches are taken down and the dumplings "picked." Since the first dumplings consumed can set a precedent for the year, certain prohibitions are likely to be observed. In silk-growing areas, for instance, soy sauce is avoided for seasoning the first dumplings because the white shapes covered with brown sauce would resemble reject cocoons, and thus be a bad omen.

While rice-dumpling preparation has now become women's work, men retain the responsibility for crafting assorted offerings from wood. Part of the rite of *koshōgatsu*

By shaving between the nodes of a long stick, a skillful craftsman can create multiple flowers on a single branch. Branches with sixteen flowers, said to represent the number of a silkworm's legs, are usually dedicated to Oshirasama, the god of silkworm farming. Three-, five-, and seven-tiered versions may also be offered at the altar of the year-god.

Opposite Sakaue Akio, a master carver of the type of wood-shaving ornaments native to the Chichibu region, decorates his altar with examples representing different crops in full bloom or fruit.

is a trip to the hills on a specified day in January to collect materials, an outing accompanied by prayers to the god of the mountain asking permission to cut in his domain. While a modern farmer may laugh away the need for such permission, he will still be sure to leave a set of offerings accompanied by a prayer for safety while cutting wood during the coming year.

The repertoire of carved wooden items is large and varies according to region. Most prominent among the carvings are the depictions of flowers or spikes of grains. These can be as simple as two wooden sticks, one with bark and the other peeled, paired to represent two varieties of millet, or as complex as an exquisite tangle of shaved wood whose long curly tufts are likened to a plant in full bloom, its head bowed down under the weight of the rich florescence. Depending on the region, the long slivers may be named after ears of rice, silken thread, or the blossoms of other locally grown crops.[6]

In addition to wooden offerings that suggest agricultural produce, farmers may fashion miniature farming tools, ritual implements for the Little New Year breakfast (chopsticks and sticks for stirring rice gruel), images of the wayside deity (honored both as the community's sentinel and as a symbol of fertility), and rustic wooden swords. The swords, a talisman against evil spirits, are placed at the

altar, in the *tokonoma*, and in the toilet or privy (the spot where people were once considered the most unguarded and vulnerable to accident). Other symbols of good fortune and fecundity are made according to the fancy of the maker, and the activity may even become a source of friendly competition among neighbors.

The origin of the shaved-wood decorations is unclear, but sources of the Heian period (794–1185) suggest that the use of the wooden flowers on ceremonial occasions was established as early as the ninth century. The decoration's strong resemblance to the cult sticks used by the Ainu of northern Japan suggests they may have derived from the shamanistic traditions of Northeast Asia, and quite possibly functioned as a sacred staff in rituals before the use of paper became common. According to a mid-nineteenth century account, flowers made from wood shavings were once popular in the cities as well as in the countryside. In Kyoto and Osaka the decorations, purchased from peddlers, were hung in front of the homes of samurai and government officials when the pine and straw ornaments of the official New Year were removed on the fifteenth; in the capital of Edo, they adorned the entry gates of commoners as well.[7]

In the parts of Japan where *koshōgatsu* is still celebrated, the decorations that have been in place since

大当

大当の神

も二コク働く者に常に離れぬ

九十お雪沼石爬自省訓

Top left In the Isoda household, even the *kura*, or store-house, is considered to have a guardian spirit worthy of a wood-shaving offering.

Top right A rustic decoration in a field in Saitama Prefecture represents a prayer for a plentiful yield. The paired wooden segments are named *awabō* and *hiebō* after varieties of millet, once an important element in the Japanese farmer's diet.

Bottom A decoration of shaved wood is often combined with an offering of dumplings. Wood-shaving ornaments were once popular throughout Japan, but as the younger generation moves away from farming the number of individuals who practice the craft is rapidly declining.

Opposite In parts of central Kyushu, sprightly balancing figures are part of the Little New Year display. Standing on carved offerings representing ears of grain, their arms are weighted with rice cakes. The paper circles in the corner, targets in a sacred archery ritual, act as charms to protect the household.

before the beginning of the year are taken down and replaced with wood-shaving and rice-dumpling offerings just before the Little New Year. In addition to the entryway, every location that is thought to host one of the household deities is likely to be decorated. The most careful attention is saved for the special altar of the year-god. Once it was common practice to hang a movable altar in that corner of the main room that lay in the year's lucky direction—a direction that changed annually according to a cycle based on yin-yang cosmology and was determined by consulting the kind of old-style calendar still distributed by Shinto organizations. As affluence has made inroads into village life, this altar has mostly become fixed in one corner so that the remaining space can be given to a television set or other fixtures of modern living.[8]

The house and its environs thus refreshed, the family quietly awaits the mystical night to come. Given a full moon in a fair sky and the intrinsic purity of the white rice balls and pale wood-shaving ornaments mellowly reflecting the moonlight, the dim farmhouse (in the days before electricity) would have seemed imbued with divine beauty. The celebrants must have heard the rustles and whispers of invisible spirits who wafted into the house on a gentle breeze. Such, in any case, is the idyllic image the exquisite setting inspires in the mind of a modern audience.

DIVINING THE WILL OF THE YEAR-GOD

The rituals of imitative magic practiced around the time of the Little New Year seek to invoke the blessings of nature, which the year-god personifies. But even the faithful may seek further assurance about prospects for the year ahead and attempt to ascertain the will of the deity with a wide variety of divination rituals.

Competition is one vehicle used by the year-god to make his will known. The contest that remains the most widespread is the boisterous tug-of-war, pitting village teams against each other to determine which will be blessed with the more abundant harvest. In a coastal community, the teams might represent sea and land, and the results taken to forecast whether the catch of fish or the agricultural yield would be better. Today's tug-of-war is a tamer event, performed mainly as a source of local entertainment, but in many areas the competition still adds color and excitement to the koshōgatsu celebration.[9]

The year's prospects can also be foretold by simpler means, in the privacy of the home. The process might involve interpreting the appearance of twelve beans roasted on the hearth to predict each month's weather, or forecasting crop conditions based on the quantity of mold coating a rice cake placed in a mortar. By far the most common

In the Tama district west of Tokyo, the ritual objects carved for the Little New Year may include wooden pull toys and guardian figures. The log figures, always used in pairs for their fertility symbolism, may be found near the entryway, at the altar, or in front of the storage shed.

An offering to the spirit of compost is erected each year on this steep hillside in Saitama Prefecture. Without the intervention of the gods, such marginal land could not be expected to provide a good yield.

practice, however, centers around the rice gruel served as a ceremonial breakfast on January 15.

Boiling grains into gruel is a primitive style of cooking that was common in earlier days. Since rice was once scarce and precious, however, such grains as millet and barley constituted the usual ingredients, with grueled rice reserved as a special treat for festival days only. Known as *mochigayu*, or full-moon gruel, the dish was associated with the Little New Year celebration from at least the ninth century and is mentioned in the travel journal *Tosa Nikki* under the entry for the fifteenth day of the first month, 935.[10] Eating rice gruel at *koshōgatsu* was once standard practice in both urban and rural areas. Reporting on Little New Year customs in the urban centers of Kyoto, Osaka, and Edo (Tokyo), a nineteenth-century observer recorded that a bean-and-rice gruel was eaten for breakfast in all three cities. Apparently the simple food was not much favored by the sophisticated Edoites, however, and many resorted to sprinkling sugar on the gruel to make it more palatable. Today the custom has virtually vanished from the cities, and even in the countryside only the most traditional families continue to prepare the special breakfast.[11]

Rice is more than Japan's cardinal crop—in Japanese mythology it is treated as a sacred gift bestowed by the Sun Goddess. This makes it an ideal vehicle for divination. At

The Little New Year custom of carving miniature farm implements expresses the farmer's indebtedness to his tools as well as his prayer for continued reliable service.

one time it was common for community members to gather on January 15 to conduct a ritual based on the preparation of rice gruel. Participants would insert a number of hollow sticks of bamboo or straw into the gruel, and when cooking was complete would judge their luck by the number of grains or amount of moisture inside the tubes.[12]

Individual farmers may do the same at home, often substituting a pair of special wooden sticks for the bamboo tubes. The sticks are split at one end and are used to stir the rice gruel, which is usually mixed with red beans. While stirring, the farmer may chant a lucky incantation. ("One grain multiplied ten thousand times," for example.) When the cooking is done, he judges his luck in the coming year's farming by counting the number of rice grains adhering to the gruel sticks, or by whether or not a red bean or two is caught in the fissured ends. Afterwards the gruel is served both to the year-god and to family members, who partake together in a communal feast. This ritual meal was undoubtedly the highlight of the traditional koshōgatsu celebration.

Taboos that still surround the consumption of the full-moon rice gruel betray the meal's symbolic importance. For the communion meal, family members may use special unpainted chopsticks that will either be set aside as talismans or broken and burned afterward to prevent reuse by someone not partaking of the sacrament. It is especially

Ritual objects carved by Sakaue Akio for the Little New Year include gruel stirrers, large chopsticks for the year-god and the family, a sword to guard against mishap, a miniature mortar and pestle, and log bundles representing sacks of various grains.

The tradition of eating rice gruel on Little New Year dates back a thousand years. After the gruel is cooked and the stirrers inspected to divine the luck of the coming year's crops, portions are offered at the altar of the year-god and to the wooden logs that represent guardians of the gate.

important not to blow on the gruel, no matter how hot it is, because blowing suggests the strong winds of the fall typhoons that can wipe out a rice crop just before harvest. Although no one takes the association literally, this latter prohibition remains remarkably persistent in rural areas.

The stirrers used to cook the gruel are themselves thought to be imbued with spiritual power. The sticks may be brandished to threaten trees into bearing more fruit or erected as sentinels in the paddy field to guard the supply of water to the rice seedlings. But their most colorful use is as a magical fertility device to induce pregnancy in childless young women. What must have begun as a folk practice with phallic overtones was adopted early on as an amusing game at court and provided the usually sedate court ladies a once-a-year excuse for mischief. The eleventh-century writer Sei Shōnagon presents a vivid picture of events on the day of the full-moon gruel festival, when women of the imperial household gleefully chased each other (and the occasional unsuspecting male) to deliver a surprise whack to the backside. Though increasingly rare, the practice persists in scattered areas throughout the country.[13]

VISITS OF LUCKY GODS IN DISGUISE

Another communal event derives from an ancient belief that certain gods of good fortune (not necessarily identi-

fied with the year-god) would visit in disguise at the Little New Year. They would go throughout the village at night, knocking at doors and demanding hospitality. If treated graciously, the gods would bless the family with good luck; if rejected, their curse would last for generations. A dramatic presentation of this belief is the Namahage, a rite observed in certain villages of northern Japan (see photo, p. 84). Young men dressed as demons in straw coats (the traditional traveling garb of the *kami*) barge into each village home, brandishing mock knives and hatchets to threaten punishment. The head of the family is obliged to receive the wild intruders cordially, and offer them food and sake. In other parts of the country children or youths dress themselves as strange birds or disguise their faces with kerchiefs and go door-to-door collecting *mochi*, sweets, or money. Variants of the practice are still found throughout Japan, but because the custom tended to degenerate into begging, it eventually fell out of favor and disappeared from many communities.

Scholars have puzzled for years about the meaning of the divine guests. Most feel their return each New Year symbolized a new infusion of life and energy in the world. Their annual visits revitalized the spring, guaranteed rich harvests, and promised to put to rest any evil spirits that might threaten the land. By welcoming the disguised

Gruel cooking is preserved as a communal rite in the Chichibu village of Fujikura. Hollow bamboo sticks are cooked along with the gruel, then split apart and inspected. The number of grains or amount of moisture inside is interpreted to predict agricultural conditions in the coming year.

Opposite Because the spirit of the roadway (*dōsojin*) is the protector of those on a journey as well as a guardian god of the community, straw sandals worn by travelers were once a common offering. In Minami Yato (Yokohama), new sandals were hung at the local *dōsojin* shrine on January 14 as part of the Little New Year celebration. The tradition continues today in the form of a 10-foot sandal (*waraji*) crafted yearly by local residents. The *waraji* offering symbolizes the community's hope for health, safety, and abundance.

guests and sharing with them food and sake, villagers brought themselves in touch with the world of the divine and opened themselves to good fortune.[14]

THE *KOSHŌGATSU* BONFIRE

One Little New Year observance that may be growing rather than declining in popularity is the community bonfire that occurs on the evening of January 14 or the morning of January 15. This festive event, rooted in ancient fire festivals, also provides for a ceremonial disposal of the New Year decorations. The bonfire is known as *dondoyaki* ("dondo" fire), a name that is said to derive either from the sound of exploding bamboo or from the nonsense syllables of a children's song. First a large conical structure is constructed of bamboo poles, to which New Year decorations of pine and straw, collected from neighborhood homes, are added. Once the tower is set ablaze, the bamboo chambers begin hissing and cracking, shooting cinders high into the air. Just as the structure appears ready to topple, boisterous youths may charge forward to try to direct the fall in the year's "lucky direction." Onlookers roast *mochi* and dumplings in the bonfire—consecrated in the flames, the ritual food is said to guarantee good health.

An array of giant straw sandals lines the entryway to Haguro Shrine in Fukushima. New sandals are put up in February to approximate the date of the Little New Year observance under the old lunar calendar. Footwear is considered an appropriate offering to welcome gods who have traveled from afar.

More often than not the bonfire will take place at a boundary of some sort—along a riverbed, near a prominent crossroads, or at the village border. Since the border traditionally represented the entry point for unwelcome spirits carrying disease and blight into the community, it was the logical place to mount a defense. Such sites are associated with the guardian *kami* (known as *dōsojin* or *sai no kami*) responsible for the community's protection, and in many communities (especially in eastern Japan) the bonfire is part of a festival known by this deity's name.

Torioi, "bird chasing," a playful children's activity of the Little New Year, also involved a bonfire. Youngsters would go from house to house singing and making loud noises to drive out the birds that would later peck at the rice crop, demanding rice cakes for their efforts. Their booty would be taken to a straw hut where they would feast, play, and perhaps spend the night; in the morning the structure would be set ablaze. The birds of summer, of course, were safely out of the way and quite untroubled by these antics, but as a form of magic to protect the fall harvest, the ceremony formerly had great symbolic importance. In many areas once known for *torioi*, the songs related to "bird chasing" have now been forgotten, but a children's gathering with a bonfire will still take place.[15]

Some trace the origin of the *koshōgatsu* bonfire to the Chinese New Year practice of burning green bamboo

In Shiga Prefecture in central Japan, community members in traditional garb pass under a newly erected *shimenawa* hung at the entrance to the village. The *koshōgatsu* rite is designed to summon a deity capable of repelling evil spirits. The use of a sacred rope to protect a community is an ancient practice, and ropes identical to this appear in some of Japan's earliest picture scrolls.

(later fireworks) to scare off evil spirits. Others link the custom with a ceremony of the medieval Japanese court, when the emperor's first calligraphy of the year was burned in a bonfire coinciding with the full moon.[16] But many scholars argue that the practice has its roots in an indigenous folk rite that antedates Chinese influence. Pointing to the striking resemblance between the Little New Year's celebration and the Bon festival (celebrated precisely six months later, at the time of the full moon of the seventh month) they contend that the purpose of both was to call home the spirits of the ancestors, to join with them in a communal feast, to divine their will concerning prospects for the months ahead, and to send them off on the flames of a bonfire. According to this theory, the full-moon observance of the first month retained its Shinto character, with the ancestral spirits eventually fusing into the figure of the year-god, while the festival of the seventh month became colored with Buddhism, a faith imported from China.[17]

Numerous traditions have merged in the custom of the *koshōgatsu* bonfire, and their interpretation is complicated by the dual nature of the Japanese New Year observance. From the point of view of the January 1 celebration, the bonfire marks the end of the holiday, the time when the decorations that provided lodging for the year-god are gathered together and burned to send off the deity for

An offering of buckwheat noodles and a lucky *daruma* accompany a Little New Year display of rice-flour dumplings. In many parts of Japan the dumplings are referred to as *mochi* "flowers," but in Chichibu, an area once known for silk cultivation, they are affectionately called "silk cocoons."

Opposite The Namahage demons burst into each home, menacing the women and children with a foil-covered wooden knife. Terrified youngsters, admonished for their past misbehaviors, quickly promise to mend their ways. Placated with offerings of sake and rice cakes, the gods dance off into the night in search of the next house.

another year. In the context of the Little New Year observance, however, the bonfire on the fifteenth can be taken as a welcoming signal inviting the year-god to descend for the celebration thought to commence with the full moon. Within either tradition, the fire rites of the New Year serve a common purpose: to exorcise evil from the community and, through purification, to transform a negative force into something positive.

The increasing popularity of the *dondoyaki* celebration may derive from nostalgia among older Japanese seeking to revive some of the cherished customs of their childhood. Many communities where the practice had once died out now actively promote the event, both as a way to pass traditions on to the younger generation and as an activity that re-creates the comforting sense of village solidarity lacking in modern life. While such efforts do attract more participants, they also reflect a shift in focus from a event usually organized by and for young people to a more structured adult-driven activity.

The celebration of *koshōgatsu* began to wane in 1873 when the Meiji government replaced the centuries-old Chinese calendar with the Gregorian system. Traditions changed slowly at first because even the confirmed modernists of the new government had to show respect for such time-honored annual observances. An 1870 ordinance did

recognize the Little New Year and a number of other seasonal celebrations in the list of official holidays, but three years later this ordinance was abolished and new state holidays—all centered on worship of the emperor—were declared.

The majority of Japanese were farmers, to whom politics was alien. They continued to follow the old calendar for the sake of sheer convenience in their farming and daily life and paid only perfunctory attention to the new holidays dictated by the state. The conservatism and intransigence of the countryside exasperated administrative officials, whose frustrated comments appear in reports issued well into the twentieth century.[18]

The venerated agrarian tradition collapsed before the magnitude and speed of changes that Japan underwent after World War II. Rational thinking and technical efficiency are the ideals that reign supreme in the country today; mystical beliefs and faith in benevolent spells have vanished.

Or so it seems on the surface of life in contemporary Japan. At the subliminal level, the Japanese still think and act as farmers, and cling to a concept of national identity that springs from the countryside. This is evident in the mass exodus from the cities that occurs at the New Year and Bon, when the whole nation seems drawn by the lure of the

furusato, or "old home town." Another potent symbol is that on the grounds of the Imperial Palace in the heart of the megalopolis Tokyo, the Emperor continues to grow rice. Official announcements of planting in the spring and harvesting in the fall, reported in the press without fail, cannot help but remind people of the ancient myths that trace Japan's agrarian roots to the age of the gods.

In 1948, January 15 was revived as a national holiday, but with a new purpose—the Coming of Age Ceremony for those who have reached the age of twenty. Friends and classmates gather together for a program sponsored by local governments, and young women, who often dress up in kimono, are likely to have a portrait suitable for matchmaking taken. In the celebration there are vestiges of the belief in fertility rites and recognition that good luck burgeons on an auspicious day. But perhaps the young celebrants should be reminded that the gods of good fortune may work their magic better in the light of the full moon than under the glare of a fluorescent bulb.

NOTES

1. For information on the Chinese calendar and the manner in which the start of the New Year was calculated, see Note on the Japanese Calendar on page 11 and Nagata Hisashi, Nenchū gyōji o kagaku suru (Analyzing annual observances) (Tokyo: Nihon Keizai Shinbunsha, 1989), 2–3, 39–48. The widely accepted theory that the ancient Japanese celebrated the New Year at the full moon is based on an analysis of texts and seasonal observances of a later period, since no written records exist to document Japanese customs at the time the Chinese calendar was introduced. One reason the imported calendar was resisted by farmers is that it reflected climatic conditions in northern China and caused discrepancies when used in Japan. Not until 1684, when a Japanese astronomer succeeded in adapting the calendar to local conditions, did the official calendar become more widely used.

2. Hashiura Yasuo, Tsukigoto no matsuri (Festivals of each month), vol. 3 of Minzoku mingei sōsho (Collected works on folk customs and folk arts) (1949; reprint, Tokyo: Iwasaki Bijutsusha, 1966), 128–29; Suzuki, Nihon nenchū gyōji jiten, 194; Sakurai, Japanese Festivals: Annual Rites and Observances, 20.

3. The Gregorian date corresponding to the Japanese New Year shifted within this period depending on the phases of the moon and whether an additional (or thirteenth) lunar month had been added to the previous year, as was done periodically to adjust the lunar calendar to the natural seasons.

4. Hashiura, Tsukigoto no matsuri, 11–12.

5. See Hashiura, Tsukigoto no matsuri, 142–43; Itō Mikiharu, "Rice Rites in Japan Proper and the Ryukyus: A Comparative Study," in Folk Cultures of Japan and East Asia, Joseph Pittau, ed. (Tokyo: Sophia University Press, 1966), 37–55; and Michael Jeremy and M. E. Robinson, Ceremony and Symbolism in the Japanese Home (Honolulu: University of Hawaii Press, 1989), 83.

6. The simpler paired decorations are usually known by the name awabō/hiebō (both types of millet), while the more elaborate shapes are called kezuribana (shaved flowers), kezurikake (shaved hangings), or hodare (hanging ears of cereal plants).

Opposite The New Year's decorations of pine and straw are burned in the purifying flames of the Little New Year bonfire at Matsunoyama in Niigata Prefecture. Children's first practice calligraphy of the year is added to the blaze to assure future writing skill.

7. The classical poetry anthology *Kokin Wakashū* includes a ninth-century poem (Book 10, #445) inspired by wooden flowers attached to a plant. See Helen Craig McCullough, ed. & trans., *Kokin Wakashū: The First Imperial Anthology of Japanese Poetry, with Tosa Nikki and Shinsen Waka* (Stanford, CA: Stanford University Press, 1985), 106. The Edo-period description is based on an account by Kitagawa Morisada, *Morisada Mankō* (A miscellany by Morisada), Asakura Haruhiko and Kashikawa Shūichi, ed. (1867; reprint, Tokyo: Tōkyōdo Shuppan, 1992), 4:95. See also Kadokawa Shoten, ed., *Zusetsu haiku daisaijiki*, 26.

8. Most newer homes have no provision for a special New Year altar, so the year-god is instead honored at the *kamidana* ("god shelf" or standard Shinto home altar).

9. The tug-of-war is associated with New Year celebrations in many parts of Asia. It is mentioned in a sixth-century Chinese source as an event occurring annually on the first day of spring. See Moriya Mitsuo, ed. and trans., *Keiso saijiki* (Annual events of the state of Chu), a translation of *Jing chu sui shi ji* by Zong Lin (Tokyo: Tōyō Bunko, 1982), 58–59, and Kurabayashi Shōji, ed., *Nihon matsuri to nenchū gyōji jiten* (Dictionary of Japanese festivals and annual observances) (Tokyo: Ōfusha, 1983), 291.

10. McCullough, *Kokin Wakashū*, 274.

11. Kitagawa Morisada, *Morisada Mankō*, 4:95.

12. In Chichibu this communal rite is still performed at a neighborhood shrine by villagers of Fujikura, Ogawa-machi. Bamboo sticks labeled with the names of different crops, the months of the year, or any of a number of other concerns related to farming are cooked along with the gruel and then split apart to reveal the oracle. A respected village elder interprets the results, which are then recorded and distributed to residents as a guide for planning cultivation. A formal version of the same rite constitutes the most sacred annual ritual carried out by the priests of the large Mitsumine Shrine in western Chichibu.

13. Suzuki, *Nihon nenchū gyōji jiten*, 199–200, 202–203, 240–41. For the Heian period account, see Ivan Morris, ed. and trans., *The Pillow Book of Sei Shōnagon* (New York: Columbia University Press, 1967), 1:2–3.

14. *Namahage* refers both to the festival and to the demon-gods who make an appearance then. Because the etymology of the name is unknown, it is difficult to translate. For a discussion of the Namahage and other disguised-visitor observances, see Yoshiko Yamamoto, *The Namahage: A Festival in the Northeast of Japan* (Philadelphia: Institute for the Study of Human Issues, 1976). In Japanese, see Origuchi Shinobu, "Tokoyo oyobi marebito" (The shadow kingdom and divine strangers), *Minzoku* 4 (1929): 203–264; and Kadokawa Shoten, ed., *Zusetsu haiku daisaijiki*, 5:183, 186–188.

15. A good description of *torioi* is found in an early nineteenth-century account by the writer Suzuki Bokushi. See *Snow Country Tales*, Jeffrey Hunter with Rose Lesser, ed. and trans. (New York and Tokyo: Weatherhill, 1986), 249–252. In northern Japan, the children's "huts" are igloos carved in the snow. Kadokawa Shoten, ed., *Zusetsu haiku daisaijiki*, 5:183–85, 214–215.

16. The bonfire at the imperial court was known as *sagichō*, a name that is still used in many parts of Japan when referring to *dondoyaki*. The ritual is mentioned in thirteenth-century diary of Ben no Naishi, but the custom of adding the Emperor's calligraphy to the fire appears only in texts of the Muromachi period (1333–1568). Kadokawa Shoten, ed., *Zusetsu haiku daisaijiki*, 5:189–195.

17. One of the early supporters of this position was the folklore scholar Yanagita Kunio (1875–1962), whose argument is put forward in *About Our Ancestors*. Tanaka Giichi, however, doubts Yanagita's theory, pointing to the absence of divination rites in the observance of Bon. Tanaka Giichi, *Nenchū gyōji no kenkyū* (Studies on annual observances) (Tokyo: Ōfusha, 1992). See also Laurence Caillet, "Time in the Japanese Ritual Year," in *Interpreting Japanese Society: Anthropological Approaches*, Joy Hendry and Jonathon Webber, ed. (Oxford: Journal of the Anthropological Society of Oxford, 1986), 31–47.

18. Carol Gluck, *Japan's Modern Myths: Ideology in the Late Meiji Period* (Princeton, NJ: Princeton University Press, 1985), 87.

IV

The Japanese New Year

Transitions, Festivities, and Religion

Ian Reader

VISITORS TO THE MAJOR JAPANESE CITIES at the New Year would likely find things little different from any other urban center in the world during an important holiday: the normally frenetic streets are empty, shops and businesses are closed and shuttered, and even most restaurants offer nothing more than a poster with a New Year greeting and an apologetic notice indicating when they will re-open. Should the visitors stumble upon a street leading to one of the city's larger shrines, however, they would find themselves in an entirely different world, enveloped in a sea of noise, and jostled by thronging crowds either pushing their way toward the shrine to pray or wending their way back clutching newly purchased lucky charms or other religious objects.

For if Japan as a whole takes a rest at the New Year, its religious institutions and their surrounding precincts spring to life, becoming the center of public activity for the first three days of the year. This is the period when it is customary for most Japanese, usually with their families or close friends (or, as is increasingly common among the young, with a special New Year's date) to make a first visit of the year to a Shinto shrine or Buddhist temple.[1] The purpose of this first visit (known as *hatsumōde*) is to pray for good luck in the coming year, to acquire lucky talismans

"Demon-quelling" arrows *(hamaya)* serve as good-luck charms.

Opposite A stream of people climb the steps of Kamigamo Shrine in Kyoto on New Year's Day. During the first three days of the year most Japanese pay a special visit to Shinto shrines where, with families and close friends, they pray for good fortune in the coming year.

and symbols of divine protection, and perhaps to have one's fortune told to see what the coming year might bring.

Prayer and visits to religious institutions play a prominent and visible part in peoples' lives at the New Year when there appears to be an outpouring of religious sentiment and behavior. *Hatsumōde* is certainly the most public part of the New Year's celebrations, and many observers are liable to conclude that religion lies at the core of the holiday. But the *hatsumōde* practice also illustrates how religious celebrations and practices are closely tied into— and may be inseparable from—the social calendar and the social and cultural lives of most Japanese. Juxtaposing themes of family, entertainment, travel, and leisure with more overtly religious concerns is a prominent feature of Japanese culture and religion, and one that is readily on display at places of worship during the New Year's period. In the shrine and temple courtyards that host stalls featuring food, trinkets, and games, worshipers often appear as interested in these distractions as they are in sending their prayers to the gods.

Hatsumōde is an occasion for dressing up, for going out and being seen, and this aspect of public display and making an impression clearly motivates many shrine visitors. Young women, in particular, dress up, either in fashionable Western attire or a traditional kimono, and

Two young sisters in their best holiday kimono pose for a photo on the grounds of Kamigamo Shrine in Kyoto.

Opposite New Year shrine visits offer a special occasion for taking commemorative photographs. Here a youngster tries her hand with an instant camera.

Hatsumōde visitors to Yasukuni Shrine in Tokyo flock to booths where lucky arrows, votive tablets, and an assortment of amulets and talismans are sold. A significant portion of shrine income comes from sales made in the first week of the year.

Opposite Two young women seem pleased with the contents of the divination oracles (*omikuji*) they have just drawn. Though people may not take the fortunes very seriously, purchasing an *omikuji* at the start of the year is a popular ritual. Optimistic predictions are said to heavily outweigh unfavorable ones.

create such demand for new hairdos that beauticians rank with priests and shrine officiants as among the busiest people of the season. Young people often travel from shrine to shrine with close friends, making the most of being seen and of seeing others. The first shrine visit provides young couples with a fashionable occasion for a romantic date, which may include visiting a shrine whose deity is renowned as a god of love or for *enmusubi* (joining two people together romantically).

For families, too, the first shrine visit of the year may be a social occasion, the time when all the members go as a group to pray for prosperity and happiness. While they are bound to acquire a charm or two to place in the home as protection against bad fortune, most family members are as likely to see their visit in terms of social and cultural custom as they are to consider it a specifically religious practice.

The activities at shrines and temples are the most visible and public dimension of a longer series of events and rituals that commemorate the ending of the old year and celebrate the beginning of the new. Like *hatsumōde*, some of the related activities are acted out in overtly religious terms at religious institutions, while others are more clearly secular in nature and setting. In many respects the religious festivities that greet the New Year between the night of December 31st and January 3rd are sandwiched

between two more secular sets of practices: those that see out the old year, and those that welcome the new.

All of these activities are in some way concerned with transition and renewal, and all, whether religious or secular in setting, have a religious aspect. The rites of transition express themes of purification, in which the old is swept away and any bad things associated with it are symbolically eradicated. They express the importance of renewal, and of remaking the world in an ideal sense (for it is also common for people to accompany their prayers and aspirations with resolutions of starting afresh or of improving themselves in some manner). Social ideals of solidarity and the sense of cultural and corporate identity that strengthens the social bond may be expressed in familial terms, by spending time with relatives; through participating, along with millions of their fellow Japanese, in the *hatsumōde* practice; or through company-sponsored rituals in which workers reaffirm their allegiance to their firm and to their colleagues.

GOODBYE TO THE OLD:
SOCIAL FESTIVITIES AND RITUALS AT YEAR'S END

December is one of the two great gift-giving times in Japan, the other being during the hot summer months. Stores are full of displays of presents suitable for employers, superiors, employees, neighbors, or anyone with

A festival atmosphere prevails as throngs line the steps leading to a popular shrine on the first day of the year. When worshipers finally reach the main altar they will toss some coins in the offertory box, clap their hands twice to summon the gods, and make a prayer for health, safety, or good fortune in the coming year.

Opposite top A cluster of colorful New Year decorations enlivens a vendor's stall. The paper decorations will be inserted in a pair of small porcelain containers designed to hold a sake offering at the household altar.

Opposite bottom One paw upraised, the other clutching a gold coin, the *maneki neko* (beckoning cat) is a popular mascot for merchants, restaurant owners, and others who rely on a steady stream of customers. Though basically a secular figure of good luck, *maneki neko* are sold at the stalls set up around shrines and temples at the New Year and, like other lucky objects, are customarily renewed annually.

Opposite Shrine and temple stalls are often filled with roly-poly *daruma* dolls. Depicting the founder of Zen Buddhism, who lost the use of his limbs after years of motionless meditation, the figure symbolizes determination and the attainment of a goal. Popular custom dictates that old *daruma* be burned at the end of the year and replaced with an even larger figure.

Left Purchasers buy eyeless *daruma* and paint in one eye, filling in the other only when their wish is answered.

whom one needs to maintain or improve social relations. The protocols of gift-giving are rigorously, almost religiously, followed and the practice is fueled by the generous year-end bonuses Japanese businesses give employees, making December a month for spending money, for shopping, and for excess. It is also the month when people busily prepare New Year's greeting cards (*nengajō*) that are sent to friends, acquaintances, business colleagues, customers, and anyone else with whom one has any form of social or commercial relationship.

The end of the year is marked by a series of actions in which the wheels of social reciprocity and relationship are oiled, in which people acknowledge obligations and social bonds and pay their respects to those who have helped them. The bonus and gift-giving season summons in a prolonged festive period of parties and social events leading up to the public New Year's holiday. The latter part of December is marked in most businesses and other work and social institutions by parties known as *bōnenkai* ("forgetting the year parties") at which successes of the old year are commemorated and problems, disputes, and tensions that may have arisen during the year are symbolically wiped away or consigned to the past. As well as providing the occasion for much feasting, drinking, singing, and letting off steam, the *bōnenkai* serves to eradicate the nega-

tive feelings of the past, allowing new aspirations to prevail.

The celebratory and partylike atmosphere of December has been further intensified in recent years by the emergence of Christmas as a festive occasion that precipitates a further cycle of gift-giving and card-exchanging. Department stores, important promoters of the holiday, are fully decorated and humming with carols by the beginning of December. Among the Christmas traditions that have been popularized in recent years are the purchasing of Christmas cakes to be eaten by the family on December 25th, and the notion, widely prevalent among young people especially in the major cities, that Christmas Eve offers the year's most romantic opportunity for a special date.[2] While Christmas in Japan is still only a peripheral event celebrated primarily with secular activities, it does appear to be gradually developing a fixed role in the end-of-year festive calendar.

The New Year period is a time for family reunions and the reaffirmation of social solidarity within the home. Long-distance trains and planes are fully booked for the rush before New Year when city dwellers head for the homes of parents and relatives living in the countryside, and for what the media describes as the "U-turn" when people start heading back to the cities early in January. It

Sake casks, donated by manufacturers from around the country, make a festive holiday display at Shinto shrines. After being blessed, some of the rice wine will be served to *hatsumōde* visitors.

has become a media ritual to report on the levels of overcrowding on the long-distance trains, and to broadcast from major railway stations with details of the preparations for, and aftermath of, this great rush.

On New Year's Eve (*ōmisoka*), the commemoration of the passing of the old year interweaves social, secular, and religious customs. It is an evening when family groups eat a special meal together and may visit a local shrine to give thanks for the good events of the past year.

The pervasive influence of television on mass culture in Japan is revealed each New Year's Eve when a significant percentage of the population remains glued to the television screen, watching the major stars of Japanese popular entertainment participate in lavish extravaganzas. Although it has lost some of its glitter in recent years, a song competition that has become a ritual of New Year's fare on television still commands as much as 50 percent of the viewing audience.[3] When the song contest ends fifteen minutes before midnight, the rites of transition shift from saying farewell to the old year toward greeting the new one. Similarly, the more private and family-oriented social celebrations of *ōmisoka* turn to more public displays that accompany the *hatsumōde* visit. The television and radio stations begin broadcasting the tolling of temple bells. Each of the 108 passions that, according to Buddhist thought,

The New Year is a popular time for people to petition the
gods by writing their wishes on wooden votive tablets
known as *ema*. Literally "horse picture," the *ema* developed
as a substitute for the ancient practice of offering a live
horse to Shinto shrines. Hung on special racks on shrine
and temple grounds, the tablets are eventually burned,
sending the worshippers' entreaties heavenward.

Above A mountain of *ema* at Yushima Tenjin shrine in Tokyo attests to the popularity of shrines dedicated to the god of learning. With crucial school and university entrance exams just a few weeks away, eager students and their hopeful parents flock to these shrines in the first few days of the year.

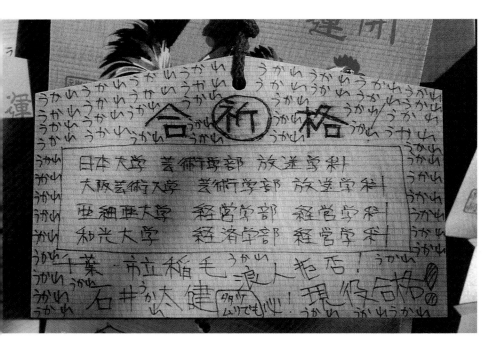

"Pass the exam!" shouts the *ema* of an ardent university applicant left at a Tenjin shrine in Tokyo on the first day of the year. After signing his name and listing the universities he aspires to, the student fills every last space with the phrase "may I be accepted, be accepted, be accepted."

Good grades, success in business, luck in love, and even a better golf score are some of the petitions written on *ema*.

Opposite The year animal, one of twelve that form the Chinese zodiac, is one of the most popular motifs found on *ema*. Shrines and temples produce new designs annually, and comparing the *ema* of different institutions is one of the pleasures of *hatsumōde* visits. This charming example was painted by Tonomura Eiichi for the year of the monkey.

hinder enlightenment is symbolically eradicated by a toll of the bell; when the last chime is struck, the hindrances of the past fall away and the old year gives way to the new.

The end of the year is thus marked by a Buddhist ritual, which sets the signal for the crowds to visit Shinto shrines. Another important characteristic of Japanese religion is revealed in this process, namely the different roles played by different, though clearly interlocking, religious traditions. In Japan the two important religious traditions of Shinto and Buddhism have by and large played complementary parts in Japanese religious life, especially in terms of the social calendar. The widely recognized Japanese pattern, summed up in the phrase "born Shinto, die Buddhist," is a reflection of this: Shinto is the religious tradition commemorating beginnings—births, coming of age, and the expression of aspirations for the future, and Buddhism is the tradition dealing with endings—death, the commemoration of what has past, and the eradication of its bad influences.[4] The pattern is clearly illustrated in New Year's practices, for while Shinto shrines are the center of the *hatsumōde* rituals and the places where people go to seek the help of the gods and affirm their hopes for the coming year, it is the Buddhist temple bell with its deep and haunting resonance that marks the last moments of the old year.

Some famous Buddhist prayer centers—such as Kawasaki Daishi in the city of Kawasaki, Shinshōji at Narita, and Tokyo's Asakusa Kannon—also attract huge crowds at the New Year, mainly on the basis of their reputed ability to answer a supplicant's appeal.[5] These, however, are among the minority of Buddhist temples, most of which function largely as pastoral agencies caring for, and performing services for, their parishioners. Such temples rarely get visitors at this time of year and, once they have tolled their bells, are likely to fall silent for the holiday period.

Seeing in the New:
Hatsumōde, Celebration, and Renewal

The *hatsumōde* period at most shrines stretches from midnight on New Year's Eve to the late afternoon of January 3rd. The largest crowds can be found on the first day of the year, but many people like to see in the New Year with a shrine visit on the night of December 31st–January 1st. In many urban areas trains, which suspend operations around midnight during the rest of the year, run all night, allowing people the opportunity to go to several shrines. Indeed, the numerous railway companies in Japan play a prominent part in the New Year's bustle by vigorously promoting *hatsumōde* visits and through advertisements for the particu-

lar shrines and temples served by their lines (often extolling the powers and benefits that such shrines are claimed to bestow on worshipers). This encourages the idea of multiple shrine visiting, and during the *hatsumōde* period it is common to see people entering a shrine or temple carrying some lucky charm or talisman from another place just visited.

By midnight on the 31st, crowds begin to build up in and around important shrines and temples. Since eradication of the ill luck of the past year, and purification in order to be ready to greet the new, are basic themes within the New Year rites of transition, numerous rites of purification may be enacted as a means of symbolically removing attachments to the past. A number of shrines, for instance, erect an arch or ring made of woven straw; passing through or under this symbolically wipes away the transgressions of the past, allowing people to greet the gods in a ritually pure and renewed state. People stand in line at such shrines, awaiting the stroke of midnight to be among the first to greet the gods in the New Year.

As the crowds build up, the shrine courtyards become alive with noise and music. People queue to approach the front of the shrine and stand before the altar where the deity is considered to reside; throwing (or hurling, if crowds prevent reaching the altar) some coins

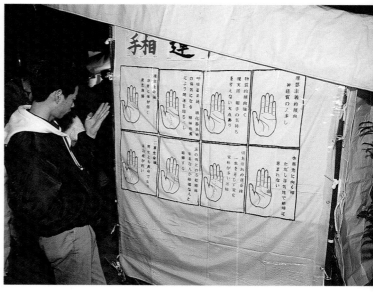

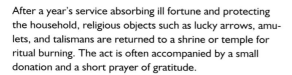

After a year's service absorbing ill fortune and protecting the household, religious objects such as lucky arrows, amulets, and talismans are returned to a shrine or temple for ritual burning. The act is often accompanied by a small donation and a short prayer of gratitude.

Palm readers, astrologists, and other diviners benefit from the popular notion that a reading of the future has special weight if taken in the first few days of the year.

into the offertory box, they bow their heads, clap their hands twice (this is the customary Shinto practice, although it is not at all uncommon to see people doing something a little different)[6] and say a prayer. Many rattle the bell rope of the shrine as an act of obeisance and as a means of attracting the god's attention, so shrines that are relatively sedate and peaceful for most of the year are filled with a cacophonous din.

In general, prayers at the New Year involve requests for protection from bad fortune in the coming year and for beckoning or soliciting good fortune. The nature of requests is framed by personal concerns and by the deity petitioned, and people make special efforts to visit a deity whose powers are related specifically to their needs. Musicians, for instance, may seek out a shrine dedicated to Benten, the goddess associated with the performing arts, while students about to take a crucial entrance examination are likely to flock to a shrine that honors Tenjin (the historical scholar and patron deity of learning Sugawara no Michizane).

The central focus of the prayers is on *genze riyaku*, this-worldly benefits. These may range from help from the deities in passing an examination, to aiding the family business, to helping a son or daughter find a good spouse, to the attainment of peace of mind through the achieve-

ment of personal wishes or through the avoidance of misfortunes. The gods and Buddhas are regularly invoked to intervene in such matters, making prayers for *genze riyaku* one of the central themes in Japanese religion. The pragmatic understanding that one of religion's major functions is to respond to the needs of people in their everyday lives is a basic feature of Japanese religious consciousness. Shrines and temples have long provided the mechanisms whereby people externalize and express their innermost needs and wishes, and seek help from their deities in achieving these needs, or at least receive the solace and satisfaction they derive from their prayers. Since prosperity and happiness are basic human desires that are closely linked with peace of mind and tranquility, it is regarded as perfectly reasonable and acceptable to petition the deities for such things. Consequently, New Year, when people dwell on their fears and expectations for the future, and when they are most concerned to set things right, provides an ideal time to visit the gods and make imprecations to them.

Included, too, in prayers for this-worldly benefits are those for *yakuyoke*, or avoidance of danger, in which the deities and Buddhas are asked to protect one from potential dangers in the coming year. This protection is especially likely to be sought by individuals who are entering what the Japanese consider to be their unlucky years (*yakudoshi*),

After their *hatsumōde* prayers, worshipers often linger to enjoy the festive atmosphere created by the many stalls set up at shrines and temples. Lucky charms, toys, and an assortment of festival foods are among the attractions.

Masks reflecting popular cartoon characters are
among the enticements at New Year shrine fairs.

Shortly after midnight, a young woman joins the throngs of those who have just paid their first respects at Yasaka Shrine in Kyoto. Her cartoon mask, purchased at a shrine stall by her boyfriend, demonstrates that prayer and play mix easily in Japan.

in particular the forty-second year for men and the thirty-third year for women.

During *hatsumōde* visits, individuals and families usually take the opportunity to acquire a number of protective talismans and symbols of good fortune that, while they may be sold throughout the year, are especially prominent during the New Year period. One particularly popular item is the *hamaya*, literally "evil-destroying arrow," which people place in their homes, most commonly in the northeast corner. This direction, the *kimon*, "devil's gate," is regarded, in the Taoist geomancy that first became popular in Japan in the Heian period (794–1185), as the direction from which misfortunes are most likely to come.

Other religious objects traditionally acquired at this time include protective personal amulets (*omamori*) for all sorts of needs—from success in education to road traffic safety—and talismans (*ofuda*) whose purpose is to protect places (such as the family house) or to bring prosperity and good luck to a place. For petitioning the gods directly, people often record their entreaties on *ema* or votive tablets, hanging them on special racks provided on the shrine grounds. Amulets and *ema* may be purchased for personal benefit, or they may be used to intervene with the gods on behalf of friends or family.

Numerous other lucky objects (*engimono*) thought to garner good fortune are sold in and around shrines and temples at the New Year. Stalls are often filled with figurines of the zodiac animal representing the new year; bright red *daruma* dolls that depict the founder of Zen Buddhism, Bodhidharma, and symbolize fortitude and determination; *maneki neko* (beckoning cats) treasured by merchants for the upraised paw that pulls in both money and customers; and figurines of the Seven Gods of Good Fortune (*shichifukujin*), a syncretic group of benevolent and happy deities usually found riding in a treasure boat (*takarabune*).

Making a pilgrimage to shrines and temples associated with the Seven Gods is a popular New Year's activity. Seven Gods' pilgrimage circuits can be found through much of Japan, but are especially prominent in Tokyo, where virtually every ward has its own course, and Kyoto, where the much-promoted Miyako Shichifukujin pilgrimage has become a thriving route in recent years. The relationship of the Seven Gods to treasure and wealth makes them compatible with both the leisure and commercial themes of the season. One well-known Kyoto department store sets up a mini-pilgrimage inside the store, with priests from the relevant shrines and temples stationed at strategic locations amidst the New Year sale racks, affording customers the happy opportunity of gaining religious merit while shopping for bargains.

The Seven Gods also help summon good fortune in another way. There is a popular belief that one's first dream (*hatsu yume*) of the year is particularly portentous, and that a happy dream heralds a lucky year. It was once common practice to place a picture of the Seven Lucky Gods under one's pillow to induce a propitious dream. Few people today express belief in this folk notion, but many of the Japanese students I taught in the years I lived in Japan told me that they, or someone else in the family, continued the custom, and I found that there was widespread interest in the nature of the first dream of the year, along with a natural preference that the dream be auspicious.

During the New Year's shrine visits many people purchase an *omikuji*, or divination oracle, which purports to tell one's fortune and offer some advice for the future. *Omikuji* are rarely taken very seriously and are usually read with amusement (often out loud to one's friends), but they reflect the underlying fascination in Japanese popular culture, expressed clearly at New Year, with attempting to predict the future. That they are sold at shrines and temples reflects the close association that has long existed between religion and divination. As a rule, after reading the *omikuji*, people tie them onto trees, branches, or to frames that at many shrines are specially erected for the purpose. Although according to popular folklore, one should tie up

unlucky *omikuji* so that the wind will dispel the bad luck, in reality most paper fortunes end up tied to the trees and fences in the shrines, for another commonly voiced piece of folklore has it that tying up lucky *omikuji* negates the effects of the unlucky ones.

This simple and lighthearted level of prediction and divination is indulged in by the large majority of New Year shrine visitors, but many people also call on a professional diviner to have their future read. During the *hatsumōde* period, fortune-tellers and diviners of all sorts—from astrologers to palmists and even, in recent years, people using computers to read palms or print out astrological charts—set up shop in and around major shrines and temples and do a thriving business.

Shrines and temples often derive a substantial proportion of the year's income from New Year sales, a fact that promotes competition and may even lead institutions to adopt charms or amulets normally associated with religious traditions other than their own. For instance, I was surprised to find a Buddhist temple in Sendai selling *hamaya*, the lucky arrows more usually linked with Shinto. When questioned about the change, the head priest replied that he was only following the lead of the neighboring Shinto shrine, which had begun selling *daruma* figures (nominally a Buddhist symbol) the year before. Ironically,

Opposite Pilgrimages to shrines and temples associated with the Seven Gods of Good Fortune are a popular way to accrue good luck and enjoy a pleasant outing at the start of the year. As a memento of the pilgrimage, worshipers often carry a plaque or booklet to obtain the stamp of each institution visited.

Above A Kyoto resident looks over his collection of *nengajō*, postcards with New Year greetings. The Ministry of Posts issues nearly four billion such cards, many with lottery numbers that may entitle the recipient to a small prize. If mailed by the December deadline, all the greetings will be delivered promptly on the first day of January.

Left "First of the year" observances are carried out with special care, since they are an omen of the year to come. The January 2 rite of "first calligraphy" *(kakizome)*, once widely observed, is now generally limited to shrines and schools. A youngster at Kitano Shrine in Kyoto concentrates on doing his best.

Many housewives who once prepared their own New Year delicacies (osechi ryōri) now order ahead from restaurants and department stores. Here a chef arranges various ceremonial dishes in a manner designed to please the eye as well as the palate. According to custom, enough food is to be prepared so that cooking will not be required for the first three days of the year.

Right Tied in colorful wrapping cloths, the tiered trays that hold special New Year dishes fill the entrance hall of a Shimonoseki restaurant on the last day of the year. A small display of pounded rice cakes in the alcove marks the season and welcomes customers coming to pick up their orders.

Opposite left On Christmas day in Tokyo, a Buddhist mendicant solicits alms across from a department store illuminated like a giant gift box. Christmas—with its gifts, ornaments, and special cakes—has become an important commercial occasion in Japan. By the morning of December 26, however, every piece of tinsel has magically disappeared, replaced by the pine and straw decorations of the New Year.

Opposite right Because the New Year decorations help summon the fortune-bringing god of the year, pinball parlors and other establishments that promote games of chance are sure to put up an impressive display.

and somewhat to his frustration, the priest did not sell many, for most worshipers were accustomed to purchasing *hamaya* at the shrine, and many arrived at the temple already clutching their new arrows.

At the New Year people not only acquire new amulets but also dispense with their old ones, which are seen as having done their duty by absorbing ill fortune in the previous year and to have exhausted their efficacy. They are not just thrown away, however, for they remain religious objects, and hence need to be properly disposed of in a religious setting. By custom people bring the old amulets back to a shrine (not necessarily the one at which they were acquired) and deposit them in the special area set up to receive discarded religious objects, which are later all ritually burned by the priests.

After *Hatsumōde*:
Secular Rites and Religious Festivals

In addition to the shrine visits, many people make social calls to extend formal greetings to friends, coworkers, and, especially, bosses and superiors, in a round of encounters that is in many ways an extension of the obligations of giving presents and sending New Year's cards. After January 3rd, most shrines begin to return to normal, trains fill up with returning workers, and the country moves back

from holiday to work mode. The beginning of the work year is marked in many companies and other institutions by formal rituals and parties whose aim is to greet the New Year and reaffirm a sense of belonging, identity, and company spirit. Implicitly at least, these rites also remind the workers that the season of play is over and that they now must return to the serious business of work.

The ritual of *shigoto hajime* (the beginning of business) is widely observed in workplaces across the country. While the rite varies from institution to institution, a common pattern is for the company president or similar leader, standing on a podium before his formally dressed employees and flanked by leading officials, to make a welcoming speech, outlining the institution's goals for the coming year and pledging his intention to work hard for those aims. Representatives of the workers then respond with a pledge of loyalty to the company and affirm their intention to work hard for its success. The event may be followed by a party to welcome the New Year (*shinnenkai*, the parallel to the "year-forgetting party" of December) that provides another chance for affirming group solidarity in a somewhat more relaxed setting.

The return to work and its accompanying rituals marks the end of the holiday period, but the broader cycle of ceremonies, especially religious ones, associated with

the New Year continues. Soon after the cycle of New Year's rituals has ended, various other "first of the year" celebrations occur, making January one of the most active times of the year at religious centers. Many shrines and temples that have an *ennichi* or monthly prayer festival (which often coincides with a market day on the precincts) celebrate the first monthly prayer festival of the year as especially important and a particularly efficacious opportunity to pray to the deity enshrined. Such "first of the year" observances, designated by the term *hatsu* ("beginning," as in *hatsumōde*), may draw as many people as, or be even more important within certain social groups than, the New Year festival. The *hatsu* Kōbō, held on January 21 at such temples as Kyoto's Tōji and Osaka's Shitennōji, which are connected with the Buddhist holy figure Kōbō Daishi, is heavily subscribed. The Shinto deity Ebisu, widely venerated among shopkeepers and merchants, is especially popular in the Kansai region, where the *hatsu* Ebisu festivals of January 9th–10th attract huge crowds. At the major Ebisu shrines of the region, such as Imamiya Ebisu shrine in Osaka and Nishinomiya Ebisu shrine near Kōbe, the throngs easily rival those of New Year's day.

The themes of protection from bad fortune (*yakuyoke*) and of praying for help during one's unlucky year (*yakudoshi*) are emphasized in various festivals that fall around the middle of the month, near the January 15th observance

known as Little New Year. This is often the moment when the old talismans from the previous year, having spent their energy, are burnt, and the gods are petitioned for protection during the year at hand. At Iwashimizu Hachiman Shrine south of Kyoto, the bonfire is accompanied by the chanting of sacred prayers invoking the deity to take away whatever ill fortune has been absorbed by the talismans. As the bonfire burns lower, shrine attendants bring out *mochi* (rice cakes) and consecrate them with the god's power by holding them over the flames before distributing them to those watching the rite. Thus the ritual that starts by erasing the vestiges and bad luck of the past ends with the distribution of festive foods symbolizing the new. With such rituals and festivals the extended cycle of New Year events in the religious calendar draws to a close, and shrines and temples return to a more normal pace of events.

Hatsumōde, Religion, and Culture

The rites associated with the New Year demonstrate that religious motifs become especially prominent during periods of transition, when religious observances and festivities both demarcate the passage of time and give symbolic expression to people's underlying feelings, wishes, and needs. The deep relationship between the cycle of the seasons and the religious cycle of rituals and festivals emerged from the premodern agricultural calendar, in

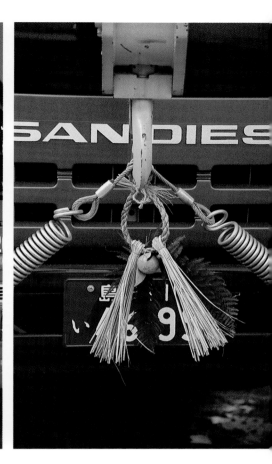

which such seasonal events as planting and harvesting were marked by religious ceremonies invoking the gods to ensure the success of human endeavors. Although modernization, industrialization, and urbanization have changed the underlying patterns and separated seasonal and production cycles, the residual influence of the old agricultural calendar continues to be strong. Seasonal observances still structure the religious calendar,[7] and the annual schedule at most Shinto and Buddhist institutions includes a series of seasonal rites, many of which are also, like the New Year, major social events.

Since the calendar reflects social, customary, and cultural influences, it is hardly surprising that many Japanese do not see it as especially or primarily religious. Even those who pray at shrines or acquire talismans at this time will describe their actions in terms that are cultural and social, more than religious. A common response to my question "Why did you participate in *hatsumōde*?" was "Because I am Japanese." My respondents, in other words, recognized that the expression of cultural identity and the performance of social custom are important elements in their participation. At a time when the whole country is at play, joining the masses in *hatsumōde* imbues people with a sense of belonging, of feeling at one with their family and fellows as well as with the wider culture within which they exist.

The number of people participating in *hatsumōde* has

Just as farmers once placed a straw offering on their tools and farm carts, so modern drivers decorate their vehicles. The straw ornament is meant both as thanks for the automobile's past service and as a prayer for continued safety on the road.

risen steadily from around 25 million in 1960 to nearly 85 million in 1993.[8] Although Japanese academics quote such figures as evidence of a rise in religious sentiment, and the number of *hatsumōde* participants is a statistic commonly used by scholars to analyze contemporary patterns of religious behavior,[9] other factors must be considered in interpreting this growth. Increased wealth, which in itself encourages the display and socializing that are part of the *hatsumōde* process; improved transportation facilities, which enable people to move around easily; and media coverage that, by drawing attention to the crowds flocking to shrines and temples, encourages people to join the throng, also play an important part. That *hatsumōde* is recognized as a phenomenon through which one gains a sense of national belonging and cultural identity is an incentive to participate. The New Year has emerged as a time when travel for its own sake has become a cultural norm, and this has further boosted the number of people participating in *hatsumōde*. Accompanying the dramatic increase in shrine visitors has been a parallel growth in the number of Japanese traveling to such tourist destinations as Tokyo Disneyland and the major ski centers, or abroad to such destinations as Hawai'i, Guam, and Australia.[10]

Statistics are subject to various interpretations. In 1989, for instance, the number of *hatsumōde* participants

declined from the previous year. Since the Showa Emperor was close to death during that holiday season and the government urged people to refrain from overt displays of festivity, the decline in numbers may have reflected national concern for the dying emperor, or it may simply have been influenced by the weather, which was generally rainy and not conducive to going out.

The number of shrine visitors grew between the 1992 and 1993 New Year periods, a phenomenon that some attributed to the economic recession which, in making people uncertain about the future and anxious about their jobs and businesses, had caused them to turn to religion for reassurance.[11] It is also possible that the turnout was affected by the good weather that blessed the 1993 New Year or that the economic downturn, by discouraging people from traveling abroad, may have increased the number of those turning to the domestic entertainment of shrine visiting.

The overall growth in the number of shrine visitors in the postwar period has been accompanied by a significant change in the *hatsumōde* experience. The current emphasis on visiting famous shrines that may be far from one's home reflects social changes that have weakened people's traditional links to local shrines and communities. The erosion of local ties has encouraged a deeper national

awareness, with the move toward prominent centers at *hatsumōde* implying participation in a national rather than local event. It also reflects the continuing growth of choice that was lacking in earlier eras when community pressures, economic circumstances, and the lack of transportation facilities committed people to celebrate the New Year at the local shrine.

Although *hatsumōde* is but one part of a cycle of New Year's activities that incorporate secular, religious, social, and cultural rituals, it is the most prominent and public of these events and one in which the vast majority of Japanese participate. Many of those who visit shrines at the New Year do not think of themselves as religious and might deny having any belief in the efficacy, or perhaps even the existence, of the deities to whom they pray. Yet each year they do go, in greater or lesser numbers, to pay homage to the gods, to carry away with them symbols of their protective powers, and, of course, to have a good time.

The rituals of New Year suggest that religious and social behavior are often indivisible in Japan. While New Year is a public holiday featured prominently in the secular calendar of the business, commercial, and economic worlds, it is also part of the calendar of social, cultural, and ritual events in which large numbers of Japanese participate each year.

Opposite The first prayer festival of the year is an important event at shrines and temples honoring popular deities. In the Kyoto-Osaka area, the *hatsu* Ebisu ("first Ebisu") observance of January 9–10 attracts throngs of merchants and shopkeepers who look to the benevolent Ebisu as their patron saint. A *maiko*, or apprentice geisha, hands out bamboo branches to be decorated with lucky charms.

Above Employees, dressed in their formal best, exchange greetings on the first day of work after the holiday. While the dress code has greatly relaxed in recent years, most institutions still observe some sort of ceremony to affirm company solidarity and establish the tone for the new year.

Right and opposite Members of the Firemen's Commemorative Guild, a descendant of the volunteer fire brigades of the Edo period, dress in traditional attire and perform impressive acrobatic stunts at the January 6 ceremony that marks the Tokyo Fire Department's "first appearance" *(dezomeshiki)*. Demonstrations of the latest fire-fighting equipment and lessons in fire safety accompany the event, helping to remind observers that good habits practiced during the New Year season set the tone for the year ahead.

Overleaf An elegantly dressed young woman stands before a mass of *omikuji*, fortune papers, tied on a rack by New Year shrine visitors.

NOTES

1. Following common practice, the word "shrine" refers to a Shinto place of worship (*jinja* or *jingū*), and "temple" refers to a Buddhist one (*tera*, *jiin* or *-ji*). As this essay shows, however, and as I have discussed in *Religion In Contemporary Japan* (Honolulu: University of Hawaii Press, 1991, pp.134–193), the activities of these different institutions overlap, and frequently, especially at times such as New Year, it is not particularly relevant to differentiate among them.

2. Limousines, rented sports cars, dinner shows, and hotel rooms are booked well in advance for this evening. This linking of Christmas Eve and dating may be an extension of the association that has been developed, largely on a commercial level, between Christianity and romance, with Christian-style weddings becoming increasingly popular because of their romantic image.

3. Known as *Kōhaku Uta Gassen*, or Red and White Song Contest, the program involves two teams of entertainers, the red team (female) and the white team (male).

4. I am not suggesting that all religious traditions always work together, that competition and conflict does not occur between religious traditions, or that the customary patterns are free of any tensions, but the "Shinto for beginnings, Buddhism for endings" pattern is followed widely enough for it to be used as a generalization. See Reader, *Religion in Contemporary Japan*, Chapters 3 and 4 for a fuller discussion of this issue and for a broader description of the functional roles of these two traditions.

5. I refer to those temples called in Japanese *kitōji* or *kitōdera* whose reputation and fame is based on the reputed abilities of the Buddhas enshrined there to grant wishes and requests, and on the reputation of its talismans as powerful religious objects that aid people in the acquisition of benefits.

6. As I have noted in *Religion in Contemporary Japan* (especially Chapter 1, pp.1–2), many people use this style of praying at Buddhist temples as well. Often

Japanese do not differentiate much in functional terms between *kami* (Shinto deities, enshrined at Shinto shrines) and Buddhas (Buddhist figures of worship enshrined at Buddhist temples), and many use the same methods of prayer at institutions of either religion.

7. The calendrical nature of Japanese religion has been discussed by western scholar H. Byron Earhart in various works, including *Japanese Religion: Unity and Diversity* (Belmont, CA: Wadsworth Press, 1982) and by Japanese scholar Miyake Hitoshi in various works, especially *Nihon shūkyō no kōzō* (The structure of Japanese religion) (Tokyo: Keiō Tsūshin, 1974).

8. This represents an increase of 240% in *hatsumōde* participants during a period in which Japan's population rose 31% from 94.3 million to 123.6 million.

9. For example, see the essays by Kaneko Satoru (pp. 77–117) and Kōmoto Mitsugu (pp. 33–76) in Ōmura Eishō and Nishiyama Shigeru, ed., *Gendaijin no shūkyō* (Contemporary religion) (Tokyo: Yūhikaku, 1988). Among other activities that are closely taken note of, and recorded in surveys such as the ones carried out by the NHK, are participation in the memorial services and festivals commemorating the dead (*higan* in spring and autumn, and *obon* in summer), visits to shrines or temples to pray in times of need, participation in festivals, and purchases of talismans and lucky charms.

10. In the first three days of January 1993, some 5.38 million people visited major tourist attractions within Japan, including 190,000 to Tokyo Disneyland (compared to 3.5 million for the country's most popular shrine, Meiji Jingū). *Fukushima Minpō*, 5 January 1993, in a report based on police figures.

11. I base this analysis on comments made on various television programs over the New Year period in Japan, in which many academics were interviewed and asked to analyze the figures, and on press reports.

SELECT BIBLIOGRAPHY

Information on the Japanese New Year is abundant in Japanese, but less plentiful in English. This list includes a selection of publications in both languages that readers may find particularly helpful. Chapter notes provide a full citation for additional works not included here.

WORKS IN ENGLISH

Baten, Lea. *Japanese Folk Toys: The Playful Arts*. Tokyo: Shufunotomo, 1992.

Bauer, Helen, and Sherwin Carlquist. *Japanese Festivals*. New York: Doubleday & Co., 1965.

Bestor, Theodore C. *Neighborhood Tokyo*. Stanford, CA: Stanford University Press, 1989.

Bownas, Geoffrey. *Japanese Rainmaking and Other Folk Practices*. London: George Allen & Unwin, l963.

Casal, U. A. *The Five Sacred Festivals of Ancient Japan*. Tokyo: Sophia University in cooperation with C. E. Tuttle, Rutland, VT, 1967.

Choe Sang-su. *Annual Customs of Korea*. Seoul: Seomun-dang Pub. Co., 1983.

Contemporary Religions in Japan, ed. "Shinto Symbols." *Contemporary Religions in Japan* Part I: 7 (1 1966): 1–39; Part II: 7 (2 1966): 89–142.

Eberhard, Wolfram. *Chinese Festivals*. London and New York: Abelard-Schuman, 1958.

Ekiguchi, Kunio, and Ruth S. McCreery. *A Japanese Touch for the Seasons*. Tokyo and New York: Kodansha International, 1987.

Erskine, William Hugh. *Japanese Festival and Calendar Lore*. Tokyo: Kyobunkan, 1933.

Haga Hideo. *Japanese Folk Festivals Illustrated*. Translated by Fanny Hagin Meyer. Tokyo: Miura Printing Co., 1970.

Hibi Sadao, ed. *Japanese Tradition in Color and Form: Pastimes*. Photographs by Hibi Sadao. Tokyo: Graphic-sha Publishing Co., 1992. (In English and Japanese.)

McFarland, H. Neill. *Daruma: The Founder of Zen in Japanese Art and Popular Culture*. Tokyo and New York: Kodansha International, 1987.

Morris, Ivan. *The World of the Shining Prince: Court Life in Ancient Japan*. New York: Alfred A. Knopf, 1964.

Reader, Ian. "Daruma: A Symbol of Good Luck." *Kansai Time Out* (January 1988): 10–11.

———. "Letters to the Gods: The Form and Meaning of Ema." *Japanese Journal of Religious Studies* 18 (1 1991): 23–50.

———. "Maneki Neko Beckons." *Kansai Time Out* (January 1986): 6–7.

———. "Shichi-Fuku-Jin: The Seven Gods of Good Fortune." *Kansai Time Out* (January 1987): 6–7.

———. *Religion in Contemporary Japan*. Honolulu: University of Hawaii Press, 1991.

Saint-Gilles, Amaury. *Mingei: Japan's Enduring Folk Arts*. Rutland, VT and Tokyo: Charles E. Tuttle, 1989.

Sakurai Tokutaro. *Japanese Festivals: Annual Rites and Observances*. Tokyo: International Society for Educational Information Press, Inc., 1970.

Streeter, Tal. *The Art of the Japanese Kite*. New York & Tokyo: Weatherhill, 1974.

Uenoda Setsuo. *Calendar of Annual Events in Japan*. Tokyo: Tokyo News Service, Ltd., 1951.

Yamamoto Yoshiko. *The Namahage: A Festival in the Northeast of Japan*. Philadelphia: Institute for the Study of Human Issues, 1976.

Yanagita Kunio. *About Our Ancestors*. Tokyo: Japan Society for the Promotion of Science, 1970.

Yoshida Mitsukuni and Sesoko Tsune, eds. *Naorai: Communion of the Table*. Hiroshima: Mazda Motor Corporation, 1989.

Fuchū City Kyōdo no Mori, ed. *Miki no kuchi: Okamura korekushon o chūshin ni* (Miki no kuchi, focusing on the Okamura collection). Catalogue of an exhibition held Sept. 13–Oct. 25, 1992. Fuchū, Tokyo: Fuchū City Kyōdo no Mori, 1992.

Gunma Prefectural Museum of History, ed. *Inori no katachi* (The shape of prayer). Catalogue of an exhibition held March 4–June 9, 1991. Takasaki: Gunma Prefectural Museum of History, 1991.

Hagiwara Hidesaburō and Sutō Isao. *Nihon shūkyō minzoku zuten* (Illustrated dictionary of Japanese folk religion). Kyoto: Hōzōkan, 1985.

Ishikawa Ichirō. *Edo bungaku zokushin jiten* (Dictionary of popular beliefs in Edo literature). Tokyo: Tōkyōdō Shuppan, 1989.

Kadokawa Shoten, ed. *Nenchū gyōji emaki* (Annual Rites and Ceremonies). Vol. 24. of *Shinshu Nihon emakimono zenshū* (Japanese scroll paintings). Tokyo: Kadokawa Shoten, 1978.

Kadokawa Shoten, ed. *Zusetsu haiku daisaijiki* (Illustrated dictionary of seasonal references in *haiku* poetry). Vols. 4, *Winter*, and 5, *New Year*. Tokyo: Kadokawa Shoten, 1965.

Kamekura Kakuko. "Nihon no kirigami: shōgatsu kazari" (Japanese paper cutting: New Year decorations). *Mingu Mansurii* (Folkcraft monthly) 21 No. 6 (September 1988): 1–15.

Kawatake Toshio, ed. *Engeki hyakka daijiten* (Encyclopedia of theater), Vol. 3. Tokyo: Heibonsha, 1960.

Kitakami City Museum, ed. *Inori no denshō kirigami* (The traditions of sacred papercuts). Catalogue of an exhibition, Summer 1983. Kitakami: Kitakami City Museum, 1983.

Kōdansha, ed. *Nihon daisaijiki: shinnen* (Dictionary of seasonal references in *haiku* poetry: New Year). Tokyo: Kōdansha, 1981.

Kumagai Seiji. *Nihon no denshō kirigami* (Traditional Japanese paper cutting). Tokyo: Bunka Shuppan Kyoku, 1981.

Matsushita Yukiko. *Iwai no shokubunka* (Culture of celebratory food). Tokyo: Tokyo Bijutsu, 1991.

Miyagi Prefecture Association of Shinto Shrines, ed. 'Kiriko' *shashinshū* (Photographic collection of paper cuttings). Sendai: Miyagi Prefecture Association of Shinto Shrines 25th Anniversary Year Commission, 1972.

Miyake Hitoshi. *Seikatsu no naka no shūkyō* (Religion in life). Tokyo: Nippon Hōsō Shuppan Kyōkai, 1980.

Miyata Noboru, ed. *Koyomi to saiji* (The calendar and festival observances). Vol. 9 of *Nihon minzoku bunka taikei* (Complete collection of Japanese folk culture). Tokyo: Shōgakukan, 1984.

Miyazaki Kiyoshi. *Wara* (Straw). 2 vols. Tokyo: Hōsei Daigaku Shuppankyoku, 1985.

Nagamatsu Atsushi. *Shiiba-mura no shōgatsu gyōji* (New Year rites in Shiiba village [Miyazaki Prefecture]). Seto, Aichi: Nagoya Minzoku Kenkyūkai, 1990.

Nishitsunoi Masayoshi. *Nenchū gyōji jiten* (Dictionary of annual observances). Tokyo: Tōkyōdō, 1958.

Okada Yoshirō. "Koyomi uranai" (Calendrical divination). In *Uranai to majinai* (Divination and conjuring), *Bessatsu Taiyō* 73 (Spring 1991): 54–61.

Okamura Kichiemon. "Miki no kuchi zuisō" (Thoughts on *miki no kuchi*). *Ginka* 45 (Spring 1981): 25–32.

Origuchi Shinobu. *Nenchū gyōji* (Annual observances). Vol. 15 of *Origuchi Shinobu zenshū* (Complete works of Origuchi Shinobu). Tokyo: Chūō Kōron, 1967.

Ōtsuka Minzoku Gakkai, ed. *Nihon minzoku jiten* (Dictionary of Japanese folklore). Tokyo: Kōbundō, 1972.

Saitama Prefectural Archives, ed. *Koshōgatsu to monotsukuri* (Ritual decorations of the Little New Year). Ōmiya, Saitama: Saitama Prefectural Archives, 1986.

Saitama Prefectural Museum, ed. *Katadorareta inori* (Concrete expressions of prayer). Catalogue of an exhibition from March 3–May 5, 1992. Ōmiya: Saitama Prefectural Museum, 1992.

Sen Sōshitsu and Sen Tomiko, eds. *Seikatsu goyomi* (Calendar of living). 5 vols. *Shōgatsu* (The New Year). Tokyo: Kōdansha, 1986.

Shufunotomo, ed. *Dentō no kyōdo gangu* (Traditional folk toys). Tokyo: Shufunotomosha, 1977.

Suzuki Tōzō. *Nihon nenchū gyōji jiten* (Dictionary of Japan's annual observances). Tokyo: Kadokawa Shoten, 1977.

Taiyō (The Sun). Special issue on the Japanese New Year. January 1982.

Torigoe Kenzaburō. *Saijiki no keifu* (The roots of seasonal observances). Tokyo: Mainichi Shinbunsha, 1977.

Wakamori Tarō. *Nenchū gyōji* (Annual observances). Tokyo: Shibundō, 1957.

Yanagita Kunio and Minzoku Kenkyūjo, eds. *Nenchū gyōji zusetsu* (Illustrated annual observances). Tokyo: Iwasaki Bijutsusha, 1975.

Yoshino Hiroko. *Onyō gogyō to Nippon no minzoku* (Yin-yang, five elements, and Japanese folklore). Tokyo: Jinbun Shoin, 1992.

PHOTO CREDITS

INDEX

Japanese words are shown in italics. Page numbers in italics reference illustrations

Envelopes for New
Year monetary gifts
(*toshidama*) deco-
rated with stylized
images of a snake, a
rat, and a tiger—
three of the twelve
zodiac-year animals.

SPIRIT AND SYMBOL:
THE JAPANESE NEW YEAR
was produced for
Honolulu Academy of Arts
and University of Hawaii Press
by Perpetua Press, Los Angeles
Designed by Dana Levy
with assistance from D.J. Choi
Edited by Letitia Burns O'Connor
Typeset on a Macintosh II
using Joanna and Gill Sans
with Berkeley Book for display
in Pagemaker 5.0 software.
Printed in Hong Kong by
South Sea International Press.